God Bless!!.

Kevin Durand

Proverbs
20:5

"Like the pool of Siloam, certain waters, like liquid words, have the power to wash and to heal. But first comes the turbulence and the waiting for the waters to stir so one might be immersed in hope and wonder. Keith Deel's poetry invites one to sit beside the waters and reflect. Whether wading in the waters or hanging on air, Deel's poems are prayers and questions, riddles and jests. This tidy little volume will offer you a cup of cool, refreshing water, that may even turn into wine in this spiritual brewery of intoxicating lines."

—Terry Lindvall, Ph.D
C.S. Lewis Chair of Communication and Christian Thought
Virginia Wesleyan College

"The title of FLUIDUS, poems by Keith Deel, speaks of water, of sources, of the endless flow of life, of the power and peace emanating from a primary element of God's creation. But when you get into the wild diversity of these poems, you find them grounded in just about every aspect of the particularities of our life here on this earth. Take note of Noah who runs his zoo and suffers from splinters; have you ever watched a one colt parade in the rain, and realized if you missed that you missed it all?; can you imagine moving slower than 'molasses in Alaska'? Deel examines our spiritual struggles, the passage of time, growing old, being young again, but always in terms of those archetypal and fleeting images that remind us of our humanity. If you are looking for hope, and also for the gentle self-deprecating delight of our trek here in this multi dimensional existence, read these poems. Read them more than once."

—Gillette Elvgren, Ph.D
Emeritus Professor of Communication and the Arts
Regent University

Words well woven bring warmth and comfort to weary souls.
Words etched in gyrating grace lift eyes toward heaven.
Word paintings of vivid emotions are grand gifts,
shedding resolute light upon too rapid lives.
Words challenge us toward ultimate realities,
fore-shadowing a journey named hope.
Keith Deel creates tenacious juxtapositions of words and life.
With humility, he slakes thirsty hearts.
His words define our relentless parade of days...
they are the touch of God's hands upon your lump of clay.

—Michael Simone, D. Min.
Author of Altitude, Senior Pastor, Spring Branch Community
Church

Fluidus
by Keith Deel

ISBN 978-1-63393-422-1

Cover design by Timo Gomez

Published by

◤köehlerbooks™

210 60th Street
Virginia Beach, VA 23451
800-435-4811
www.koehlerbooks.com

FLUIDUS

KEITH DEEL

VIRGINIA BEACH
CAPE CHARLES

FLUIDUS

. . . for he has founded it upon **the seas**

and established it upon **the rivers**

Psalm 24:2 ESV

ACKNOWLEDGEMENT

Sometimes I feel like a canvas with an array of artists placing their brush of color upon my mind and emotion, painting rich and moving scenes as part of their everyday lives. I am blessed to have been surrounded by so many spectacular souls naturally inspiring and motivating me to places I would have never known apart from them. I am grateful for their lives, words, songs, sermons, laughter, love, and grace. I would like to say "thank you" for all you have done and how you have painted my life with your colors. My desire is that you find some reflection of yourself in the words and emotions of *Fluidus*. I know we are there together.

Letha—the love of my life and the song of my heart, my inspiration; your voice is pure beauty as angels quiet to hear your orchestra, leading souls in songs of praise.

Keeley, Bayla, Charis, & Keenan—rays of light breaking through cloud, stars brightening the night, gifts from our Father and the motivation for all I do.

Cecil & Dawn—you gave your lives away for others and taught me the meaning of love. I am forever indebted to you for eternity in my heart.

E. G. & Myrna—selfless in your love for others, early risers, and your stories, the funniest I've ever heard.

Michael & Gail—creatively communicating to my mind and heart for over 20 years, vaulting God's Word "across the skies . . . warming hearts to faith," Psalm 19:6 MSG.

Gil & B.J.—You are artists for the artist; your faith and works are beautiful expressions of God's beauty.

Daniel Forrest & Paul Putt—you grew my love for literature and opened my mind to T.S. Eliot.

Bono & U2—immeasurable inspiration, bottomless depth, and the soundtrack of my life.

Ravi Zacharias—God's human library of eternal thought, your gift opens my heart and mind to the language of meaning and redemption.

Artwork by Bayla, Keeley, Charis, & Keenan Deel
Cover design by Timo Gomez
Photograph by Caroline Cashion

INTRODUCTION

"The river is within us, the sea is all about us."
T.S. Eliot, *The Dry Salvages*

I have always been intrigued by water, with its movement and flow, the rise and fall of the tides and the power mighty rivers and raging oceans generate. I love the peaceful serenity of a quiet mountain stream and the howling growl of a secluded waterfall. Water, it is in us all, without it nothing on Earth would exist. It is where first life came into being and it affects our lives in countless ways. It is fluid, ever moving, ever changing; rising over enormous boulders and dropping deeper into the greatest depths found on Earth. It moves in ways we do not understand and carries forward civilization's souls, dreams, cargo, and supply. Water brings life, and then death. It is a friend and then the enemy we fear. My most peaceful and turbulent times have been on the water, and our deepest questions in life are like rivers flowing to the sea, always looking for a way; sometimes floating, at times swimming, other times roaring, and then, at times, drowning.

It is in the puzzle of living this flowing journey that truth is honored by doubt as the known is surrounded by the unknown. Questions are one of the most consistent attributes of our existence. Why? Why life, why pain, why death, all the questions of Job, why? Even if one lays hold to a faith or surrenders to a belief, the puzzlement of suffering, the vagueness of eternity and the shadow covering free will, remain on the mind and in the heart. Doubt wrestling in the daily unknown and unexplainable, takes a role beside faith, and as doubt asks, faith can grow. Doubt progresses into questions, inquiring our minds to understand the heart of mankind, with its kingdoms of potential, and the very seat of evil. This journey of floating is seen in the reflection of light illuminating from a star that shone eons ago. Shining its light on fleeting moments on the river and withering flowers on the shore. But these moments are a cradle in our lives, nurturing love, joy, happiness, relationship, and peace. And these flowers are rainbows of color over birth and achievement, over hope, over love and forgiveness, and even over death. Theirs, being the only color and fragrance on an appointed day. It is in the fleeting waters and the withering beauty that moments and colors become thoughts and memories that when written down become poetry, the *fluidus* of our lives.

We turn away to face the cold, enduring chill

As the day begs the night for mercy, love.

A sun so bright it leaves no shadows

Only scars, carved into stone

On the face of earth.

The moon is up and over One Tree Hill

We see the sun go down in your eyes.

You run like river, on like a sea

You run like a river runs to the sea.

U2, *One Tree Hill*

CONTENTS

OF BELIEF

Be still, be wise, cease striving, stop fighting, be in awe, return and know, recognize, desist, let it be, let it go, be still and know . . .

PSALM 46:10

We have to find the back door to people's hearts because the front door is heavily guarded.

RAVI ZACHARIAS

COVERING

Layers at first, warm, swaddling cocoon.
Sweet baby cheeks.
Protection as wardrobe and
snuggles as hovering, brooding.
Warm layers of life and light
lying softly over sunken valleys,
and pressing mightily against the rising
Patriarch of infant Everest,
its knees as such, wobbling to stand,
and realizing its own self, its weight, and the waiting.
Morning takes a breath and it is good.

A covering will amend, warm, brushing skin.
Sweetness and sin.
Protection as wardrobe and
hugs haunting, lonely.
Winds press into life and night,
blowing away softly, memory,
and howling into caves, expiring fires,
cooling the warmth of familiar gardens,
its trees as such, wobbling to stand.
And self realizes its weight and begins the waiting.
Evening falls in hush and it is still.

Deep under hand-spun blankets;
deep under conscience, shivers the soul.
Layers upon calloused skin;
layers thick, rest restlessly in lullaby.

When the skin peels, gauze and time
heal sweetness in scars.
Protection as wardrobe,
and surrender, a weapon, détente.
Enter Ecclesiastes, a depth of knowing.
Each art howling, crying in pangs.
Its inhabitants walking the circle
with bag and burden pressing down;
backs bent, and wobbling to stand.
One states your worth in weight, now waiting.
Deprivation howls the midnight, and it is chill.

As babe and armies cover to defend,
the sour forms the need.
And wardrobe as protection
rents to bare the bareness,
and all essentials rest as decoration,
cracked and falling at unknown feet,
as unwrapped gifts ordained to awe,
unpack the generation's clutter, stacked;
and wobbling with buckling knees to fall.
The weight of skin and wait of soul realizes
the darkness gives way to dawn, and it is done.

NOAH

Never been there before,
Let me stay where I am.
Obedient, righteous.
No one write about me.
So much to do at the zoo,
No time for an interview.
Living respectively of nature's laws,
Caring for life, and for lives.

Bubbling brook,
Wells and springs.
The earth's gift, surfacing.
Long walks by the river
Keep me grounded,
Let me know that danger can be washed away.
The moving filter clearing the air
As long talks with my Father
Keep me sane,
Let me know that relatives are close in pain.

Never been there before.
Clouds weighted and
Dark, angry and roar.
Wind herds the flocks
Almost human in movement,
But not what I could have ever thought.
My protection for those, not of blood,
Ones not of the promise to come.

There is work in a plan
That I do not comprehend.
Understanding the instructions,
But not what their results reveal.
I know splinters, I know hammers.
I know the density of trees and hearts.
As I sit by the fire,
The sound of a soft flowing, trickling stream
Medicinal through the night air.

The morning awakens with a circus of sound;
Braying, neighing, snorting, the disturbance
        deafeningly loud.
There is moisture thick from the ground,
But fear touches the soul to see sky water falling down.
The unknown, the never before,
The stampede of creation trying to get through a door.

I watch in amazement
As the maze of hundreds, maybe thousands
Know what they came here for.
These hands built a dryness,
This heart designed a soft spot.
Now the cavern fills with a rushing roar,
And the laughter has seemed to stop.
The years complete, an answer found in extreme.
And new questions now float,
My riverbanks washed away clean.

Never been here before,
Didn't know the sun would be swimming,
While quieted voices sometimes echo in the night.
A platform of survival, an audience of family.
My firm feet floating,
While those of obedience worry not for food or fame.
My labor, your comfort.
No interviews, I would not quite know what to say.
Rivers upon rivers deepening this cleanse.
Through water the destruction,
And the colors to begin again.

MIDNIGHT,
OUR DARKEST HOUR

Bent shoulders slumping
under the heat and light.
Man's dreams shifting
on the sands of time.
By the sweat of the brow,
bread to the plate,
As the fallen soul hangs hollow
in the dreaded wait.
Arab deserts for crossing
and drying blurred eyes.
Man moves into twilight
and cast the stars the question 'why'?

And there's silence in the darkness,
and the dark so still.
This human path to desolation,
begs the heavens for a greater will.

And then midnight becomes our darkest hour.

Now thirsty for the answer,
the barren senses the blood's pour.
And generations of old
feel the rise of a celestial tour.
A star explodes with light,
traveling the night sky with news.
Shepherds quake, the wise awake,
and the Revealed is among the few.

The stable straw scene surreal,
and the heavens open with glorious song.
Eden renovated by love elated
with the answer waited for, for so long.

It came upon a midnight clear,
when our darkest hour and greatest fear,
chose to surrender to Divinity near,
That chose to come upon a midnight clear.

WEIGHT AND BLACK CLOUD

Weight and black cloud, uninvited, have made their way
     to this scene.
But the door was propped open by a boot worn down
traveling back from curiosity.
Now though here safely, and passage through the
 arch a requiem,
baggage begins to arrive from destinations unimagined,
with desert mirages packed so neatly within.
A stranger, now a guest, resting comfortably by
     the low embers glow.
The curious conversation but once, now there is so much he
     seems to know; and familiarity bonds the friendship of
     the fallen former foe.
To have never travelled there, is almost always on the mind;
questions, regrets, the push of pride,
bring yesterday and tomorrow to eternal infinite.
Now the garden is a grind, seems to slowly die with each day
     of work; the soil, the seed, and the water they need,
seem to be tainted in some way as a result.
The curious trip and the knowledge gained
have regressed into a slow sloped ravine.
The evenings quiet, and coolness cold;
I embody all that is around me,
as youth lives out its zest on stages of Sock and Buskin,
while the wings hold all things old.
The wrinkle of time appears as a slow smile would
while watching children grow.

Weight and black cloud bring down the
     grandest Olea europaea,

its trunk twisted and uniquely gnarled.
Its time endless, millennial, but now known as
    what used to be.
So many decisions made under its branches;
so many questions uprooted in its fall.
It is the first of many friends to disappear,
and each passing making confusion clear;
that this falling, aging, dying is known
in the flow of fountains, and moves from water to blood,
permeating the inner fibers with fear.
Who will be next? What tragedy will fall?
A family broken by brothers at the altar with an
    offering of war.
Brokenness and silence, uninvited, have made their way to
    this scene, but the door was built with the freedom to
    know love's choice.
And now the wandering through destinations unimagined,
leaves the heart and water and blood dry like the desert,
dry to the decaying bone.
Hope is wrinkled in time
across the unkept promises to children now grown.

Weight and black cloud, carried to this scene
from beyond a garden waterfall;
from before dust was made flesh and wrapped around soul.
On a journey eclipsing cosmic origin,
before beginning and molding and brooding;
existing pre-light spoken into light and word spoken
    into all things. Weight in the decision, and black
    cloud in the celestial drama of proclamation of

pride by the beautiful one through his song.
This commitment before lightning fell and burnt into the
    heart of compassion the outline of full victory through
    surrender;
carved a path for completeness through choice,
knowing that it must be severed as server to the return,
and full knowledge of the wholeness that brokenness brings.
It is carried, weight and dark cloud,
to that garden of twisted and gnarly Olea europaea;
its fruit for life, its oil for healing, its wood for stretching
    out and holding all promises true.
Now the blood and death that fell in all gardens is weighted
    and blackened to this one, with this one, and under
    this tree.
The weight drops blood as sweat,
and dark clouds cover slumbering slaves,
and swords being swung for naught,
and cloudy and cold and muddy the dirt kiss
and stench of burnt breath boiling from the fallen lightning,
which carved into man's heart the space for death,
its grip tethered in every umbilical cord.
And now under this tree all things are known,
just as under the beginning tree
all grievousness was invited into knowledge,
and the release of a journey from decision opened the
    floodgates of, on the one side, love, and the other
    side, blood.
Death caught in the middle and fulfilled,
and pushed down through the temporary tomb
and into and through the heartlessness of hades,
carving into all hearts the insignia of kin and King.
Decision, knowledge and journey now eternal.
And weight and dark cloud, the only reminder of
all things ancient and temporary,

wait by the door, as the going out and coming in of
curiosity cured in the covering of sin,
gives way to water and light, and the blood
to all children to begin again.

Mammon

Gold melded melting,
dripping with each beat
of a heart.
The value weighed in the art
of baited breath beside
the emptiness of full cans of trash.
Or, stacked neatly, rowed
and counted at Pharaoh's feet
as endless efforts exist
to create a golden bliss.

A slave to one power to another,
only free in the slavery of choice.
It beats, it melts,
the universe itself
and the self of existence,
heavy as the bullions
that weighs down the spirit of flight,
and the freedom that might
raise hands as trees
and draw all life to its knees.
In the courtship of worship,
the bride to the groom in offering.
Though the gifts to exalt are
maimed in the walk into mirrors,
they see the disease
eased into lines
on the face of a race
less human with time.

The outside grows larger,
barns to build and fill,
while the inside grows darker,
complexity in free will.
The soul bottomless.
The thirst quenchless.
The weight heavier than hands
could ever carry,
and it pushes
through,
piercing the skin,
rasping the bone,
freeing the blood that flows to atone
and the sixth level gold
becomes unknown
in a system where surrender
gets you the gold
but the mammon that's prized
is what keeps you in the hold.
The beating heart of life
and deadly weight of gold.

Solomon's triple sixes
overlooked in the system,
but the one he loved reminds
how valuable the mixed grain.
In perspective, the moment,
in retro, the regret.
Plan for there, and free the here.
Wrap your arms for now
and watch it disappear.

BABYLON

Worn down
like a dirt road
Under the weight
of an overload
Potholes
deep in the soul
But maybe
you still need a way home

We have crawled
upon this dust
Bled the gravel
from these cuts
Slept the ditch banks
and the ruts
But maybe
it's the way home

Much too tired
to go to sleep
To give up
doesn't bring relief
All that can
doesn't satisfy
And when all alone
Love asks, 'why?'

Now Nebuchadnezzar
has consumed the grass
Modern Babylon
a thing of the past
And Eden's still covered
like a dirt road
The weight of wrong
an overload

Deserts turn men
in circles of oases
And garnish their souls
of familiar places
While the fire-sword burns
warmth stirs the soul
Heat to the fruitless
while blind men find their way home.

THE WAIT

I have given up days for you, and you wait for me.
My tongue sticking to the roof of my words,
thoughts in remission, finding lines in reflective glass
that cut into the day
reminding us this is not the past.
The waiting is the living in the giving up of days,
and to have the day offer a benediction
of irises and violets and rue, a baptism of blossoms,
gifts of memories waiting to be introduced
at a table of hearts warm with a life of friendship
which fails not in its surprises.
Being there with a decoration of smile,
and an accent of tears is miracle enough
as repayment of the waiting,
which is not considered debt by any measure.
The sweetness of patience is savored in the soul
just as the aroma from the handcrafted culinary artwork
of thanksgiving drifts through the air of conscious blessing.
It rests deeply in the moment
cementing weeks and months of waiting
into a single afternoon of realization, and comfort,
        and *echadh*.

Each awaited feast invites an uncanny truce with the future,
one in remembrance of one no longer waiting.
I give up days for you and you wait for me,
like the tug that needs resistance for meaningful existence,
and I the grand Courser or Tuscarora,
larger than life in the mind,
never fully in reality and never fully leaving it.

And then you show, as you have always shown,
though compliments of doubt are thrown at you
like shouts at the moon covered by cloud.
You're there, and tides move, blood circulates,
laminin holds all things together,
and there is an eye in the storm.
A passageway, a door
through which one can go home,
to a place they've never been.

OF MEN AND GOD

God incarnate
becoming man.
An argument in essence
some say it can't.
Krishna, Gautama,
Muhammad three,
all God sent
but whose Son is He?

No longer sing unto yourself
The "Song of the Lord."
Stop the jihad,
the death in holy war.
I am the Tao, the Truth
and the life vehement.
There is no God but God
and who is His prophet?

Action without attachment as
religion in the motion
of action not taken
is a real seed from
which a real tree unfolds.

Moksha
Salvation
Release
"Every man can be a Yao or a Shun"
"I give you life and that more abundantly"

Commit to the five duties
or count the cost.
To start life and die
leaves a tear to be lost,
([Tears of "Why hast thou forsaken me?"] for you)
And lost is where all were
as the plow was offered
in a kingdom
with a new start,
in a new song
with love heart
Selah!

MARY

In that place of peace
that seems
just out of reach
wanders my soul.
All that you have given me,
All I have ever known.

My hands open, empty,
into the air.
You take from me essence,
and weave your Spirit there.
All that I've experienced,
all that I will ever see,
can't create a thickness
to keep your blood from me.

Spinning in circles,
spirals inward winding,
to steps unfolding and
bridging water to find me.
With the image in breath
whispered by Spirit,
the Eternal to time,
to live to redeem it.

And life
comes to my soul.
I try
to not lose control.
And why,
you've replaced all I've ever known.
You've searched and searched,
now God finds a home.

S
  H
    E
  L
L

I see God in the twisted shape of a shell
  In the spiral mystery of layers, color and detail
    In the smooth and rough, sharp and blunt
      In the calm to adapt and weather the storm

      Wrapped with the wind, a tornado within
      Water and cloud and earth's ocean stream
      Washed in the salt, polished with sand
      Whistling waves echoing in a child's hand

      I'm fixed on its beauty, the visible is only part,
      And transfixed on its existence as a masterpiece of art
    I see God in the twisted shape of a shell
On the peaceful shore presented by water, storm and gale.

Hanging on Air

Hanging on air,
the morning mist,
a crying earth's prayer.
In the pain,
a life remains.
In the pangs,
a child again.

A billion have crossed the room,
new colors, new tunes.
Satellites of thought
painting new moons.
Twice, not a number
But experience.
Hope, not a chance,
but deliverance.

Twelve for the world
of doubt,
of denial.
To fail.
Love for the world,
the sun, heat,
the heat,
hell.

What we can do
has already been done.
The photos fading,
the slowing run.
The hills now smaller
and harder to climb.
The grapes now withered
beside baths of wine.

And you slip into a mountain,
or a deep sleep.
Surrender is the winning
and not the retreat.
The earth takes you back
and the Spirit, your soul.
The earth's prayer, a morning mist,
and the hanging air, cold.

KINSMAN

Some days dreams
Some days desire
Some days, days in the maze of the liar
But for the life of me, for the life of me
Some days higher

Some plans made
Some plans changed
Some plans played out in life's other games
But for the life of me, for the life of me
Some plans the same

> Why you took what wasn't yours
> And turned it to something more
> Left reason dead at the door
> And for the life of me, for the life of me
> Made it yours

> And you, there on the moor
> For me, I wasn't sure
> And your eyes, light to the skies
> For the life of me, for the life of me
> You had to try

Some chords soothing
Some chords irony
Some chords full stanzas of hypocrisy
For the life of me, for the life of me
You chose what to see

And I stand, a body worn
Where what's human, has been born
And my cry in the night
Silent with the light
For the life of me, for the life of me
Your blood in the fight

RESURRECTION

Life, that moving flow of I don't know, lets go, I hope so.
That never-ending repetition of wanting the future every day,
till childhood ends and most of the future watches
    from yesterday.
Life, so powerful in its free will, its will to live and
    to live again.
It has endless days, the deepest dreams,
closest friends, sunsets, moonbeams.
Its days are numbered and its trouble, plenty;
its cup to be full, sitting empty.
Its pain as breath, and its stain a suit on the soul,
dressed for the dance, shivering cold.
So life meets death in its passing of the day,
and none escape this escapade.
Life meets death and death takes control,
and only it knows the bridge and its troll.
One at a time and a matter of time,
the clicking ticking creaking clock of mankind.
So it's settled, no question, life accepts it will cease.
So stack it, store it, hold it and pack it in a valise.

But know this, he would not have died had you been
    there that night,
and now there's only a burial and death at this sight.
And life knows this is the end,
to rest in peace while death decadent.
But he would not have died had you been there that night,
would not have had death overshadow his life.

"Step aside,
Roll away that stone that has set for four days,
it hardness covering a promise that I have made.
Come out helper, your help is here,
and in your life of meeting death, this will be clear;
death now meets life, and the first introduction I will oblige,
and call death by its name and put fear in its eyes.
And death will lose its grip, and its spoils be made elusive,
and sin will pass through a fountain, finding truth
    to be exclusive.
And death will bow to life, its shadow to shrink in this light,
that shines from creation's dawn and crushes the
    soul's dark night.

No, he would have died had I been there by his side.
Death would have taken him, for it is its pride.
But for your sake and for you to believe,
all moved forward, and then the reprieve.
From the fall, it is all man can do to survive,
as death rules the night and travels the sky.
But now death where is your wound, grave where
    is your win?
For now you meet life, which I have begun again."

Life met death for eons in this crime,
and now death meets life for the very first time.
And sin is crushed in Christ,
His life over death, a power shining sublime,
and radiates in our hearts
as this story becomes yours and mine.

THE LIFE OF A SOUL

I tried to absorb beauty,
its warmth lying gently on my eyes.
The oceans and landscapes,
and depth of amazement in the skies.
But when I would close my eyes
the beauty I would see,
among the dark shadows of question,
would be the soul dancing with curiosity.

I tried to stack up coins of gold,
their coolness for calmness in hands.
In buildings and in papers,
and in values of diverse land.
But when I counted on the scale
the measure that would be,
among the dark weight of balance,
would be the soul looking for reprieve.

And so then I tried to love you well.
Love's fame to be openly known.
With family and a host of friends,
and in good causes for the show.
But when I needed someone
to stand when love betrayed,
among the dark broken kinship,
was the image in which the soul was made.

And now there's no longer 'I,'
though I am privileged in this place.
In a life given, of beauty and provision,
with a family all related in grace.
And when I counted the cost,
a price I could not pay,
among a currency of sacrifice,
stood the soul's worth, with love as its name.

SON

I once had a son
my name he did take.
He sat at my table
and ate bread with no 'thanks.'

The hard winds blew
and my boy became strong.
He had desires in his heart,
he moved on, on his own.

The noise of his life
drowned my whisper in his ears.
The seconds of pretentions
filled up all his years.

Now my son cries alone
each night in his soul.
The young and innocent,
now guilty and old.

I did him no harm
as he spoke not my name.
The choice of his silence
screamed loud in his pain.

Now my boy like a Bedouin
and I like a Sage.
Echoing in the desert,
the shovel silence, a cue to the grave

The closed mouth deadly,
no word and no name.
I fall from the rafters,
through flesh into shame.

I see you in the distance,
my stare quickens your mind.
"I've been here before,
in a more pleasant time."

You say I look tired,
so weathered and worn.
I remind you of your beauty,
on the day you were born.

But now I am your mirror,
I'm what we've become.
I, a longing Father,
you, a silent son.

You've had all this time,
and I beg for what remains.
The silence, but for a word,
and son is your name.

TRINITY

There's nothing like a body
and its movement through time.
Nothing like the energy
of thought through this mind.
And nothing like a soul,
existing in chaos and control
through this drama we call mankind.

And fear and fire
and open wires
keep the blood red
in our veins.
And hope and doubt
fight it out
while desire feels
a warrior's pain.
They all wrap around
the core that is the ground,
and the dirt from where
we get our name.

And if only a circle spinning,
like a top from the beginning,
and His joy a dizzy ending;
break the body, free the mind
save the soul.

ONE COLT PARADE

Hunger wrapped tight around bone.
Torn skin falling close to the memory of home.
Love takes away the love of the game,
and money changes all except for your name.
Excess is no place for the lonely of heart;
you breathe sacred air, knowing only in part.
If gold were no object, where would you be?
Dying isn't death if it's making you free.

Footprints, footsteps,
chasing this life away.
No chance, perhaps,
it seems to slip away.
A child's hands for your plans,
do you give it all away?

We run, we run, run to be free,
into walls and holes we blindly can't see.
We hope for the chance
to change what we can't;
the music fades
and we keep the same dance.
Into the desert we carry our flood;
going to find dryness and getting stuck in the mud.

I pray rain on our parade to change the direction,
and cheer the one colt parade to carry perfection,
the one colt parade to carry connection,
to carry protection,
resurrection.

More Than
a Savior

A dying flower
in the desert
bends its face
to the ground
A petal withers
without water
drifts quietly
through the air

A fountain flows
East of Eden
jagged rocks
broken there
A smooth stone
rolls in the Jordan
wonders how ever
He got there

There's something more
that carries a soul
from your life
to the sky
He's something more
who breaks His heart
to better know
how we cry

And when the desert
feels the rain
and the water
a new tomorrow
There's something more
than the gamble
more than a promise
more than a Savior

THE CHOICE

His breath can be as hot
as a scorching desert wind,
or as cold as ice-breaking water
freezing on your skin.
He moves in a direction
that only begins to make sense
when you're lost in hot contention
and you're cut down by the fence.
Your need is what he needs
when you know you can't cope.
Your belief is what draws him,
lets him show you your hope.
There's no exit from this stage
as it spins you round and down.
He throws cues from the wings,
you stand motionless without a sound.
Turn tonight,
turn within.
It won't be from outside you,
it won't be a sin.
For love, you pay a price,
you take pain by the hand.

And love may cost a life,
to reach inside and find the man.
Sails in the distance
carry off your memories.
The wake rises around you,
draws you to your knees.
Couldn't it have been easier,
somehow, more simple in the plan?
Nothing so hard, so obvious;
you float, or walk away a man.

What Am I Dying For?

What am I dying for?
Living comes with such ease,
what am I dying for?
Let it go, let it go.
Life to the dead, let it go.

I believed in someone
and something I needed more.
They brought me fragments of life,
but what am I dying for?

If it can't twist a soul,
turn blood ice-like cold,
shatter the paradigm's mold,
is it worth living for?
To put it in perspective stages,
earn you more than deserved wages,
is it worth living for?

Unless it doesn't quite make sense
and go beyond intelligence,
it won't be to die for.
But when a cross is broken,
arms stretched out as a token,
toward a day in Eden long before,
yes that,
offers something to die for.

BORN, CHOICE, LIFE

Born
    Comfort
        Pain
    Comfort
           Trust
              Choice
        Fear
           Faith
              Choice
           Love
        Hurt
    Comfort
        Loss
           Hope
              Choice
           Desire
        Betrayal
    Comfort
        Failure
           Growth
              Choice
        Defeat
           Humility
              Choice
        Death
              Choice
        Death
              Choice
Born
              Choice
              Choice
                Born
                  Life

How Patient Are We?

How patient can you be?
How patient with me?
How you feel my failings,
how you heal my feelings.
And how long the rope,
Swings out on hope?
Hangs us over safety,
saves us.
Answers reach for my questions.
Faith bleeding through open doubt.
Brokenness floating parallel
to your heart we've ripped out.
Son of God,
Son of God,
How patient are we?
Living after death,
bound to be free.
Are these steps real
as I walk in a circle?
Or laughter for angels,
all a dress rehearsal?
I'm pulled somewhere in between,
a pendulum of extremes.
You create these dreams.
Son of God,
Son of God,
How patient are we?

So Many Things

So many things that can't be explained
An all-powerful nothingness
With such a creative bang.
That speck of dust and
Where it came from.
The vastness, endless,
Its knowledge unknown.
The age of it all,
Newborn and grown.
The pain that penetrates
What might be in each, a soul,
Beckons to accentuate
A universe bitterly cold.
And life, its randomness intricately detailed
With programmed physiology
Rivaled only by its discovery.
So many things that can't be explained
We can agree upon that.
A choice to honor and be in awe of the unexplainable,
Or to explain it away as nothing and impossible.

So many things that can't be explained away.
Man's mind and mortality.
A desire for good, a desire for evil,
Morality in the mold
And the creative concept of eternity.
The giving away of life to give life to a stranger.
Laughter and love, deceit and anger.
The prophecies of old fulfilled
In a thirty-three year span.

The hate born in the desert of one god by one man.
Redemption and grace
And evil's ever present grip,
Solidifying man's existence with choice and its
    power to admit.
Nothing ever found, nothing ever proven, nothing
    discovered, nothing ruined,
That overrides creation's conclusion, teeming with
So many things that can't be explained away.

AND THE ANGEL
KNOWS WHO

Where is the great frying pan?
Now a chosen Sabbath and where's my ham?

Dear, love, now hence.
It's been three weeks before, three weeks since

Worked through a paper cut a week today.
For polyester knees I get this pay?

Sit for a minute, for a time we know.
Pray for this moment, the pain as you go.

I'm sick of this rocker, where's my foggy tree?
Give me Jannes and Jambres, no hair-lip for me!

Write on your heart the battle cry.
Take not for yourself, but the spiritual eye.

Damn it! Get off my car, out of my yard.
I'm going in early for promotion. How about a new.... Guilt.

Under a table, in a corner, dusty floor,
"Hallowed be thy name.... AAAH." An acid cure,
     you'll see no more.

Let's go tomorrow, this time for real.
But the light steals a minute of pigskin field.

A tongue speaks in poisoned rats, while supper is in place.
The darkness brings rodent's feet fetid on my face.

                    Cough, cough, to the doctor, then to bed.
            Understand, and pity sir, it hurts my fragile head.

The dirt path leads and settles in a skull's bed.
My sockets sense the shiny steel way above my head.

                    A straight line tube and the dog moves.
                    In a sweating voice, death can now prove.

The State takes you, it's quick and it's through.
One less tongue, and the Angel knows who.

                    A satin-lined casket holds up a suited 'why?'
        Once born, in his second death, and everyone wants to cry.

Alone at the fire-funeral, and the wind blows away.
The body released a scarring hold and the Spirit wins the day.

Because it is All I Can Do (Matt)

The children laugh and run and play
And my mind goes back to another day
When innocence was part of life

Looking back I recognize the feelings
                that I now feel

The gift of life
In a spring flower
In the crispness of autumn air

          I recognize the sounds
            that I now hear

The cries of pain in growth and change
The thunder in the storm
Your tears in the rain

Because it is what I can do now

            I look back
            I look back

Men cry and walk and pray
Their minds turning to a future day
When innocence is restored in life

Looking forward I recognize
Glimpses of images

There, in the wholeness of life
The rest for the weary
In the light of His glory

I recognize the sounds
That at times danced joyously in my soul

The rewarding laughter in the completion of a task
The joy in hearing, "Well done my son"
And your voice now joining angels in crying
    "Holy, Holy, Holy"

Because it is all I can do now,
I look forward

For Matt W.

One Word Book

Branches bees beaches queen
Stories songs preaches sings
Gardens rain raising Cain
Promises milk honey pain

Slave babies freedom call
Death wind bread law
Judges warriors prophets dream
Failure spirit boy king

Songs tears battle field
Lust murder free will
Divide enslave wonder lost
Silence star announce cost

Breath spirit new above
Law fulfill El love
Possible hope blind name
Roman Jew Greek change

Greater give power praise
Eden Olivet valley range
North south east west
Freedom forgive faith test

Honor blessing voice fist
Narcissist pride selfish kiss
Rising desert sword slain
Prophet brutal god name

World collide system man
Surrounding Peace Holy Land
Last worst fallen stand
Second last coming again

Creator creation groom bride
Redemption completion banquet life
Answers sight Son man
Designer Fulfiller Eternal I AM

Dying Alive

As phones, cars and washing machines get smarter,
people are not following the same path.
Certainly educated beyond intelligence, the sense
    of the common,
now out of style, frowned upon, "My God, it's a thing from
    the past."
We came out of caves and conquered a bloody
    barbaric world,
where gods were warriors on fields of shame,
and there a god born with blood as his name.
While this god stayed true to his universal plan,
part of humanity converted more than the will,
and freed the mind of man.
Each individual; God-given rights; give up on hate, and let
    love be your fight. Through this freedom that was bought
    by the freeing of the soul,
a western world exploded with minds of gold.
Charity became currency and spent on the world well,
and dreams became visions of futures to foretell.
And this freedom was free to all who would keep it,
freedom to worship or deny completely.
This human experiment in grace was not perfect,
as human hands, when taken hold, always twist it.
But never before had such freedom been implored,
with a government restrained, the people need not fear.

Freedom, that conduit to enable, that wide avenue opened
    for the thoughts and ideas of great minds to race upon,
    the speed exhilarating, the direction, toward light and
    enablement.

The thoughts, faith fulfilled as freedom saw freedom
     grow in good,
and choice allowed itself to be right and disciplined.
A community of consciousness with restraint and respect,
rewarding responsibility, knowing freedom can loose the
     derelict.
Enter the enemy as he sees arms wide open.
Through this freedom he crafts the tools to conduct a
     cacophony of internal attacks at the base, where the
     pillars penetrate and the centuries old foundation lies
     exposed for prior purpose of knowledge,
but now as a target of a progressive plot to prove foundations
     are futile and freedom's ring only as loud as regulation
     allows.
"Did God say?" It always starts with a question, then a twist,
     then a promise, that when exposed shows the taking away
     of what is already known.
What is an attempt to add to, dilutes what is true with a
     mixing of muses, and warriors stand strong armed with
     weapons of no use.
It was from within the garden and now from within
     freedom's own ranks
that the garden was poisoned and freedom was flanked.
Now the West stands defeated in its own good graces
by a ruthless deception covering barbaric faces.
At least we have phones, cars, and washing machines
     that are smart,
as we surrender our souls to the lie evolved as
     progressive art.

A DEADLY SECOND

There, under fallen conclusion
Semi-circle
A half, un-halved
Under or over
A subtle, less interesting conversation
A trying point is given
But only spins a question
Round and round
Four hair piles
Poor waste paper files
Point, raise up brazen eyes
Intensified by rejection
Possible in the surely impossible
I will, a strength-less confession
In the human race of possession

Where is the dance?
Solid, winds break
There is a second of life
In the dance of grabbing
In depths of water, heat, storm and mud
And I grip faith
Any burden will be a wrinkle in a face
A jewel
Oh, why and cry
I must not die as another pain to my birth

An eagle flied
A king implied
And kingdoms died
It's by time, October
It falls between breath and death
Dance little one
A morning star
Dance
Star
Come

WHAT CAN I DO?

What can I do to gain your attention
what can I say to cause a response
Anywhere I move is by your direction
Anything good is by your design

If I climb the peak of Everest
If I run the greatest length
It is all under your shadow
It is done by your great strength

So I bow down in worship
And lift my hands to praise
And make the one choice you gave
To lift no other name
I'm here to sing your praises
I'm here to know your worth
To accept that I am new
Through your death, second birth

What can I do to gain your attention
what can I say to cause a response
It is worship that warms your morning
It's the surrender of my wants

I praise you
It's what I'm here for
I worship you
It's what we were made for
There's nothing I can say
And nothing I can do
To melt your heart
Except to worship you

So I bow in your attention
Sing out in your response
It is worship that warms your morning
It's the surrender of my wants

Preacher (CBD)

You are in some ways
Like a man from olden days
And you've been there before
Looking more for a side door
Words erupting from your face
And you think there is still a place
The sum, and you're a part
Fallen kingdom in your heart
You turn the key
See an old man
A sword remaining
From an outstretched hand
And words as sharpness
Your only weapon
And kingdom coming
A parson's heaven

ATONE

As molasses in Alaska
or maybe just a bit slower,
bent a scared body of ruse
as cover for another.

Deliberate in protection
its sort only of the heart.
The mind excused excuse
as memory sculpted it to art.

The crease of time
holds beauty in its hands,
and erodes all smoothness,
altering the purest of plans.

Dirt blown blithely,
then watered to mud.
Ru'ach in the lungs,
what screams to above.

All reach,
not reaching the peak.
A choice of love bleached
and the Eternal intrigued.

A choice for a lifetime,
and a lifetime to make.
Water pushes to spirit,
the wake in the wake.

WILL THE HOME TOWN RECOGNIZE ME?

Coming down from the mountain
Crossing over the sea
Going there to die
To set the homeland free

They no longer look to survive
They have forgotten the meaning of revive

How can I enhance it
Leave love to chance it
Bones twisting in flesh
Souls tangled in mesh

I fall from the mountain
I drown in the sea
With scars on wounds
Will the hometown recognize me?

What is this shimmering gold,
That weighs more than love?
Will buy you all sorts
But none from above

Out of reach tonight
It trickles through your hands
Could have opened many doors
Could have drawn you many plans

Love is lighter
When it asks you to let go
Begs for, when you're falling
And doesn't have to know

Coming down from the mountain
Drowning in the sea
Going there to die
Will the hometown recognize me?

GOD

Do not show me where to go
Do not spell out your will for me
Do not answer all my prayers
Do not react to my every plea

Do not reveal every step to me
Do not help me to always understand
Do not give me the words to say
And do not fill my outstretched hand

What I need most in this life
Is for the God who created me
To take my life in this world
And to break it like a seed

To come and rest beside me
In the coolness of the day
To be the beating of my heart
The very breath I will take

To plant me where He would
To see me develop and unfold
To use me as shade from the heat
Or as kindling in the cold

To continue His life in my veins
To have His hand reaching through mine
To hear His words roll off this tongue
And to have His thoughts fill this mind

I don't need to know were I'm going
I just need to have you there
I hand back all that is yours
And I give you this life as my prayer

OF QUESTIONS

Where wast thou when I laid the foundations of the earth?
Declare, if thou hast understanding.

JOB 38:4, 1599 GENEVA

Oh, oh deep water, black and cold like the night
I stand with arms wide open, I've run a twisted line
I'm a stranger in the eyes of the Maker . . .
Oh, river rise from your sleep

DANIEL LANOIS, *THE MAKER*

SHADOW (GETHSEMANE)

Do you sit,
as the moon sets
beyond the trees?
Do you sweat,
as it swoons,
a shadow on bent knees?

Where are you
as He waits
in the wings of the night?
Your heart beats
as His breaks,
and sleep is all you've gotten right.

The clinking quiets
as He stills
the death in your hand.
Your lips press,
what should be love,
the poisoned breath of man.

Alone, He moves along alone.
Alone, He moves, not darkened,
and by the Will.
Your eyes hollowed,
by His shadow
the only sound,
a green-winged teal.

THE BEE TO THE FLOWER

The bee to the flower,
why do you not dance?
The flower to the bee,
why do you chance?
The bee to the flower,
why do you not freely fly?
The flower to the bee,
why do you not sit idly by?

The bee to the flower,
why do you not buzz?
The flower to the bee,
why all your fuss?
The bee to the flower
why do you not sting?
The flower to the bee,
I would not think of such a thing.

Now, the flower to the bee,
why this questioning of sorts?
The bee to the flower,
why such splendor and no courts?
The flower to the bee,
why the sting to an innocent hand?
The bee to the flower,
why your color over breathless man?

The flower to the bee,
I give the life you carry for free.
The bee to the flower,
I carry to live, the nectar for me.
Why then bee, do you question what
you see?
Why then flower, can you not be the bee?

Temples and Bars

There is a temple,
profits a good people's guilt.
An altar for sleeping,
where some have knelt.
There are rumors of truth,
silver lining in lies.
There's mass for the masses,
and no tears in the eyes.

There would be no bar
if no profit from your thirst;
no altar for praying,
where some bow to curse.
Where answers run free
in stories that are told,
and those confessions bleed
from the hands you hold.

Imagery, imagery,
where would He be?
Litany commits me
to go there and see.
Thirty-three, thirty-three,
It's years south of Nazareth.
It's New York and Babylon,
Jerusalem and Paris.

It's a half times two,
and the shoot comes up seven.
It's the world in the worldly,
and the hell to get to heaven.

Dressed in the cloth,
he raises the vase as a cup;
and with the devil's mock,
his face he lifts up.
One cries for his Savior,
one cries for his shame.
One voice pierces the night,
as they scream the same name.

TWELVE SUMMERS

Skies, white and fluffy,
rolling endless in summer smiles.
No rain and no tears;
no age, and as one, in forever blue.
Deep breaths and deeper laughs,
as what life is for,
in soft fields as a cradled nest,
plays out questions
that won't be laid to rest.

What plans have you stretched across that blue promise?
What day have you taken to change all others?
This eclipse of the sun, out of sequence and rotation
These twelve summers, all that remain toward completion.

Sincere uncertainty, in this Eden intrusion,
and the inhabitant, no choice.
To the pool to drown?
To the feast to poison?
Through the bliss an arrow,
and in the soul, treason.

Skies, white and fluffy,
and forever so real.
And white and red and puffy,
metal in the deal.
Something hauntingly unnatural
in the color of that sky,
that lobotomizes every conversation,
and rests on the cleft, a 'why?'

CONFUSING ADAM

Part I

Solo, lone.
The river rolls to somewhere.
I, not even a breath,
Nothing in air
To cause a rise
None

Sleep, unconscious.
The side of the soul opens to something.
I, not able to catch breath,
Weighted lungs only exhale.
The sun, it's warmth rising to life
One

My God, why
Hast thou poured out mystery?
I, as confusion. Of me, for me, with me.
Wholeness taken from me, to ever be pursued.
Its shape, love, its fragrance, home.
You.

Part II

It was in the evening that the soul of exchange
    expired of desire,
and saw heaven's stars wink,
and its neighborly moon smile and blush.
Draping a shadowy cloud.
It was evening, and so it was Eve.

It was in the morning that the heart of desire exchanged
    eternal for expired,
and saw void's fruit taint, and its lonely companion
    knowledge, confused and hiding.
Draping a covering, in place of.
It was morning, and so it was mourn.

It was time that drew bodies exchanging nature
    for expiration,
And saw all attempts for the garden,
overgrown and burning.
Removing the drape, for full Noachian pride.
It was midnight, and so it was the witching end.

HUMAN

God, asleep on the job,
from my point of view.
But my vantage point limited
and my assessment skewed,
by the same slumbering scientist
whose experiment has gone larrikin;
whose love overcomes all,
but disputes not a masquerading harlequin.

Thanking Him daily for His benevolence,
as I am delivered from the evil,
that I was born into with no choice,
unlike the devil.
Healed from a disease;
comforted in a loss.
This disease, to be healed from?
To lose, to know the cost?

The ocean we've been thrown into
swallows its victims once more.
And for the rescue we are grateful;
redemption on a flooded floor.
But the toss, the float, the sink and the save,
are the cry, the life, the sin and the grave.
It comes out of nowhere and then returns,
leaving clues of more questions from antiquity's verse.

You reach in to move me.
Only the dirt-man had a choice.
From where you placed me.
And it taken by a more angelic voice.
I wasn't there when they were made,
nor with the Cornerstone,
but when foundations crack, crumble;
the losing human to finally know.

Your ways, not of mankind;
in first, with a fool's finish of last;
not able to hold the future
by holding to the past.
And all you want is all
that the human mind can't comprehend;
the fruit, the choice, the knowledge.
In the beginning death, life in the end.

ATHEIST'S CREED

Confused in the confusion,
the guessing in the guess.
Ignoring history's tapestry,
overlooking the obvious.

Existing in no existence,
the realm of facts not knowing.
Just here for the ride,
no beginning of the going.

Affirming a negative,
assuming all intellect:
in your theories of no reason,
and your politics of react.

Morals, and no morality;
laws, and no source.
Insanity makes more sense
than your history with no course.

I have the watch
that no one made,
as I live this life
that no one gave.

And I won't answer the question
that never enters my mind.
I know that my not knowing
is all that matters in time.

And since all is so random,
then random is Supreme.
Let's organize random,
and make it our king.

And then random will rule
in all people and things;
no future is needed,
no history to explain.

And that should answer it,
put my mind at ease.
If there is anything, it's nothing,
and I as I please.

DEVIL'S THUMB

Ego and appetite keep honesty at bay,
slipping through the chambers of the heart,
a twisted passion for self.
On the long, lonesome path, casual careless concern
is no match for indulgence, the enemy-warrior of the soul;
its aim flawless, and only disciplined by intentional
tearing away and putting on.
When presentation becomes existence,
the agape is on display but not layered into rehearsals,
being in the story as craft, but not the story as life.
Self is no escape artist and attaches with ease to its warmth.
You, yourself and yours, is and are an army of one,
undefeatable from without, and tamable only from within.
It is with the mind that the heart moves
and the two speak separate native tongues,
speak with rampant emotion and calculated conviction.
To the victor, not always the spoils,
the spoiled not always victorious.

Does self lose and venture to its longing,
that, though not seen, is known in its stillness
and whispers in the quietest of times;
the times that only war can present,
after the tearing away, before the putting on.
Self, the vilest of enemies, once war-worn and tamed,
can be that eternal friend;
that coming home, that surrender and loss of everything
       uncontrollable, now malleable

by the image which reflects itself in all surrendered souls.
Does it meet itself in that image and flow to its wellspring?
Its attachment pulls, tears and weeps to know,
in the stained and brokenness, is the weight of appetite
    and ego.

I Am, In a Name

I have seen this world you shaped
Known the soul a breath you gave
Colors, circles intricately laid
Underlying light caverns a universe of dismay
Minute to massive
The atom to the split
All life held there
And the power to destroy it
Though the physical be obliterated
The spirit, a breath it takes
Though death, the sleep of man
In the soul, mankind awakes

Why the mystery? To nurture faith?
Why the waiting? To patiently wait?
And then the suffering? The human fate?
To be given, so to be given away?
To return as citizen to a foreign place?

In the mystery, the time.
Daughters of Zion, Sons of Cain,
The answer to existence,
I AM, in a Name.

Thunderbolt & Respite

Are you angry? I feel the heavy thickness in the air I hear it
roar and rumble, and finally crack open with a grand and
deadly light that splits a day sky covered with the color of
coal, releasing all that dust has gathered, throwing it down in
rejection, or as offering. Do I read this mood swing correctly,
as it always brings some fear and some concern? Just like a
conversation with an uncle who easily found my faults, and
instilled fear and concern into my endless summer days.
Is it anger I sense and see in this behavior, holding every
opportunity for punishment or random destruction, as is not
your nature, but is our reality?

Are you happy? The thickness of the air has subsided,
having been pushed down into the ground by billions of
liquid bullets. The rising sun smiles on the horizon, and
the landscape grins back with reds, yellows, greens and
blue. There can exist no trouble in this troubadour's song
of morning. Do I read this change of heart correctly as all
feels new and at peace? Just like a grandmother who knows
nothing but the beauty of a soul, making me feel new and
at peace. Is it happiness I see in this behavior, holding every
opportunity for joy or random kindness, as is your nature,
but is not our reality?

QUESTIONS

What is the shape of void?
A circle?
Existing
From your mind to soul?

What is the color of question?
Fading blue?
Gray, Dorian Gray
Painted under eyes for you?

How deep is doubt,
Now falling?
How deep
Into belief does it go?

How hard the ground
Of knowing?
Waiting there
on the bottom below?

How much does it cost
To let go?
Lose control?
Say we don't know?

How much does the heart
Hold
Of giving?
Try to empty it through living?

What can we know,
more than Solomon?
A riddle?
A larger castle to die in?

How old hope?
Our Father
In time?
And hope to introduce Him?

SUBDUE YOU TO RANDOM

I have attempted to subdue you   to random,

     and now I am ?confused??   as to   wh y.

Why random over ORDER

for all things,   except   my   life?

I require strucTURE in my existence, my sur – vival & mind.

I inscribe laws to insure An o r d e r l y humankind. Only

from education,   a medication for this   life,

       fragile in its shell.

And always a compass for safe travels...*...to avoid some type of,

       heLL.

My randomness??   huh, huh huh !!

I labor endlesssss   to   make sure it doesn't   ExIsT.

MY ORDERLINESS, THE top priority IN A universe OF

       listlessnesssss.

       I want the cosMOS in chAos,

its purpose a nihilist flOAt.

And itself, its need for life, but its   *SOUL*,

        the best human   *JOKE*.
        Now how can these two egregious

be side by
 side,

                        the oNe wHo can't explain, perfect,

and the oNe not understood, derelict?

To take what I don't knOW   and dismiSS it to
obsolete,

        while being surprised by what is my show
and the similar beings I meet,
            is backwards   going   forward,

and its sense not made,
                    I fully admit,

and now my structured hypothesis impenetrably fit

        around a random iDEA
            I have crEAted
            only to forgEt.
            I forget there's…. nothing there, the only
fullness is my life,
where I have aTTempted

to subdue you   to random,

        AND NOW I am confused ?? AS TO WH y.

To Know Not

I tried to hold it in my hand
A few were saying 'Let it go'
I tried to learn all that I could
And the few were saying
You already know
But the child today, tomorrow is grown
And what was held in comfort
Could have been sown

Is part of the purpose
Not to know?
And the part of dying
What makes us grow?

And I believe
Only what I can
A thorn in the side
The essence of every man

Silence His strength
As he speaks it again
Thru eons old truth
I understand that I can't

So in the surrender
Strength is shown
And by not knowing
A little is known

Not complete
In between
And looking around
For what cannot be seen

Then to know fully
Now to know what?
To admit I don't
And accept I might not

LESSONS

Have I taught you, my child,
to be busy enough?
Too much on your plate,
not enough in your cup?
Has selfishness been displayed
while I have been away?
Have you learned to hold in
all the things you need to say?

With many rooms to run in,
have I given you a place to hide?
Through the walls, hear the voices
of those we've pushed aside.
Have you learned love without risk,
the kind that doesn't cost too much?
The safety of keeping your distance,
the art of staying out of touch?

Can you grieve in the loneliness,
an acquaintance taught me so well?
Did we decide the end of the story,
then somehow refuse to tell?
Have I taught you to die,
surrounded by all that is life,
and grace funerals for hollow men,
with guests who cannot cry?

If I have bequeathed you
these hard lessons so well,
You've absorbed a way to die,
earned degrees in how to fail.
And I have never known you,
seen your face, touched your soul.
But cost you life's sweetness
and shortened your road to growing old.

I will clean a little off my plate,
reach down to take a child by her hand;
Try to know some of this life together,
not always needing facts to understand.
Let's row a little closer,
out of the current, to the shore.
We'll slow down this life a little
so we can live it a little more.

To the Right of Me

To the right of me are the fruit
>   Hanging from branches just out of reach
The rewards, each with its name
>   Written within an idea of what it could be
And the names blurred and distorted
>   Leaving only guesses as to what wishes are
So nothing in the unknown is different in what it is
>   From the appearance of what is known
And the reach for what waits one inch or a lifetime away
>   Is only known by the pain of distance
So the pain comes not from injury, from falls, from pushing down
>   In that without a dimension to, not heal, but avoid the necessary
>   Healings
And the lowness has never reached so high to cracked glass
>   Swaying slowly with enticing promises broadcast
>   Through faulty connections and buzzing speakers
And the smiles reflected in the efforts
>   Are out of contact with what is unknown and hoped for
And are results of the simple faith in reaching
>   For what one believes will answer the definition of reward
This eye of happiness in the storm encircling, exists ignorant that Movement in any direction
>   Is to become closer to what voids the expectations of the feeling

THE OLD MAN

Are you forced by circumstance to do
what you do not desire?
Are you coerced per chance by truth
from the lips of a liar?
Who has been to the garden
and planted the seeds so well?
Now weeds are choking the flowers
and the gardeners wait by the well?
Something is happening tomorrow
with the nails still stuck in a tree.
There are seven reasons to die for,
but one reason to be free.

How many Christmas mornings
will bring their gifts for free?
How many Easter Sundays
will the Son rise in the East?
How many second chances
does a man get to take?
To make the right choice the first time,
to say he made a mistake?
I don't know when it's coming,
And lies laugh at where it's been.
But truth is denied on the portico,
unprotected and hemmed in.

Who has asked for a sign,
and refused to look in His hands?
Who has looked for a God,
but not into the eyes of a man?
Something is happening tomorrow
with the nails still stuck in a tree.
There are seven reasons to die for,
but one reason to be free.

REPAIR

I am going to the doctor
I have been feeling a little ill
Then to the lawyer
To set straight my will
I have an appointment with the accountant
To correct a mistake in the books
Then to the surgeon
To correct a mistake in my looks
I went to a counselor
To discuss shortcomings in my life
He knew every one of them
Like he had talked to my wife
But what can I do
With this canyon in my soul
It echoes a void
And shadows a God-shaped hole
There's someone to fix
My yard and my car
Someone to stretch skin
Over these scars
I'm repairing my life
To fulfill that which is my role
But where can I go
To fix a tear in my soul?

FINDING YOURSELF

If you are looking to find yourself, I don't think you will find you here, though these salty islands bring you peaceful comfort, they do not bring you.

If you're looking for someone else, they're everywhere, but if you're looking to find yourself there, it won't be in any of them, it will not be you.

If it's in pain, a hug, a song, a laugh, that you look to find yourself, they only introduce you, introduce you to yourself, as they know you but they are something else.

You stand in a circle, body, spirit, mind, and stretch your heart in longing, as human, to the Divine. In no place or person, pain or comfort, but in your trinity you are defined.

Look for yourself there, in the embryonic weaving of all made new, leading to movement, conscience and thought, a river of you. Within it you live, a flesh-wrapped soul, eternally unique, one of a kind, from a single-purpose mold.

WAITING

Through the trees
Your eyes sparkle
in the night.
In the breeze
your breath warms
love tonight.
And you wait.
How long do you wait
for children running,
clinging to their pain?

I've seen tomorrow
and somehow
we are all there.
A little closer
to knowing
that for which we cared.
And you know,
how long did you know?
Your children going,
and where did they go?

Through a man
you reach for me.
In His hands,
a place to bleed.
And we wait.
How long do we wait,
in the hazy confusion
that moves
to outline
your face?

WHO DECIDED?

Who decided the right way to treat your brother?
What step of evolution requires a father and a mother?
Who made the earth an altar and an object of worship?
Where in nothing, is found this great compass?
If the answer is out there, has it been among us?
Can random chance of chaotic confusion present morality?
And what if I am my brother's keeper but he's not
        keeping me?
How do you present existence as nothing and that
 not a hoax?
And love a fictitious demon in imagination's desire to boast?

So life is attached to the 'fable's' result of love and sanctity,
While the 'fable' is ignored and denied in the shadow
        of a tree.
You'll hold tight to mercy, and forgiveness a must,
And squeeze survival of the fittest alongside your
        adoption of trust.
How do you balance so well one of the two extremes?
One of nothing randomness, and one that explains all things?
A smorgasbord of delicacies, and you choose the ones
        that suit,
But then you make fun of the host and lay claim to the
        sweetness of The fruit.

Deceived, maybe blinded, then again a choice you may
        have made,
To enjoy the rules of engagement of a game you will not play.
So on the outside of completeness, your realm of halves lay
        broken Down.

You toss the jewels and ride the swine, and refuse the bow
    worthy of The Crown.
There can be no more confusion than to long for love,
    knowing it is Remiss,
And no more human the error to accept that the Divine
    does not Exist.
Without the answer, there is none,
And your mockery a loaded gun.
What you hold dear, the epitome of irrelevance,
and the seared existence, a mirror of your conscience.

So who decided the right way to treat your brother?
If you or your brother, then freedom changes that to another.
You cannot have the ultimate decision and no
    decision maker,
and beg for your bellies bread and insanely wish away
    the baker.
How foolish are you in all your knowledge of this
    your existence?
You magnify armies of pressure to walls and marvel at
    the resistance.
Your heart gives way to your mind, as a nursery of
    babbling fools,
and you think you draw from great nothingness, a set of
    human rules.
Well luck to you and karma too, you have no keeper of truth,
and creation rules godless fools, and your kings become
    your zoo.

OF PAIN

The world is so vast while you're living,
so small when you're dying.

"April is the cruelest month, breeding lilacs out of the dead land,
mixing memory and desire, stirring dull roots with spring rain."

T.S. ELIOT, *THE WASTE LAND*

BETRAYED

When your warm dreamy sleep
ends in an ice-cold shiver,
and soft, familiar comfort
floats on a flood-cresting river...
When the sky is clear
and lightning cracks the center,
and the warmth of summer love
is frozen in sudden winter...
Betrayed

You said love rolls
like thunder in the sun.
Seems now that happiness
is the warmth of a gun.
So you pull the canons
onto the cold portico;
aim them recklessly,
maybe just for show.
Firing edges and pieces broken,
where a dream used to be,
and with tears tearing as bullets
you turn love into the enemy.
Betrayed

From heavens white chambers
looking down on what's bent,
you flinch into broken,
through the human element.
And ask of no man
what you wouldn't give
the pain of betrayed,
and the cost to forgive.
Who walks through the fog,
distant, wounded and dazed;
who's forgotten the meaning,
and tries to forget your name.
Betrayed

NOOSE

Bound, woven, tied, corded;
crafted with its purpose in hand.
Yarn by yarn,
as a web spun, not in haste,
and hangs invisible till surprised face
and hands react in swarm.

Skin over breath, separated,
both flush and taint.
Air from life, dissected into trees,
with arms raised as rejoicing leverage.
Not executed and loosely encircling,
noose, with its desire in wait.

No cessation, but a threat imminent;
a pedestal to reach spoils.
A step toward them, a swing.
So standing respite, chin high and lungs full,
daily in truce bondage, with freedom
one step, to noose tightening.

Some crack of timber,
some knife of deliverance,
some flood of cold release from
that human hold of dominion,
violent in its uninvited mercy,
and noose woven fails to appease.

If only the chance arose
for exit of this bound ship;
from the noose intact, and not enacted.
From still to movement,
knowing it brings frozen pain;
those of nooses, memories.

But to die like Sampson,
taking down what you can't hold up;
strength, sight and the fable, love.
Success is death in accomplishment,
and passion, the rope from the tree.
Pedestals and fibers broken, down to above, and free.

DECEIT

Winds blow in
the mist of deceit.
A canyon howling
under its frozen retreat.
And chill-bent hands
carry cold blood-laced truth,
that drips into a cavern's cup
on the table of the liar and the sooth.

The path is lone,
and you the same.
Your lips say one thing
and your mind another name.
Not quite the brightness
without the dark.
The spirit renewed willing,
gives way to weakness of heart.

Wounds can be many,
death's blow but once.
Breathing the air of belief,
as it devours the dream façade.
Stay to watch it fall?
Or crumble under it all?
The fight is gone,
quiet the song,
black the dawn.

TO BUY A DAY

Fallen, broken chairs
Splintered words spoken without care
And night falls
And love is gone
How much to pay
To buy a day?

Through a glass the sand
Like water through your hand
"The way of a woman with a man"
There is no pay, there is no pay
To buy a day

To fall in a moment
Without being attached
And to fall for love
Is illusion attacked
The picture bigger
Than you in a mirror
And stones fall
From crumbling walls
Run from the inside
To the open tonight
To the open night

If you give it all away
All the words you can say
There is no gold you can weigh
Nothing you can pay
There is nothing you can pay
To buy a day

Jesus Barabbas

Eyes sunken, entrenched.
Vision focused, only as random
as the discovery of a star
on pitch, as waves roll ashore.

Hands clenched, scarred.
Open only for thievery,
to crush; losing the grip
on spoils, elusive as they are.

Conscience morphed, seared.
White iron, hammered unrecognizable,
till reason as treason, maps
out a wide highway, your own.

Heart, granite, beauty.
Bewildered, petrified weight.
Breaking every chamber pure.
A hollow cavity echoes the pulse.

Soul, distorted, question mark.
Stained, lacking color.
Radiance amuck, rainbows mock.
Shaped void, outlined in eternity.

Human, all encompassed in loss.
Divine, incarnate, skin.
Ru'ach reaches, spirit breathes.
Free the blood curse, bleeds.

Barabbas, already dead.
Freed, He in his stead.
Barabbas, all men in you.
Vulcan's fire cool, proof.

Steps under feet anointed.
Crumbling earth's kingdom, frail.
Truth renders truth asking.
King, none but Caesar, the will.

Eyes fixed, rays of light.
Hands a missile, holding quaking atlas.
Conscience, an arrow, split apple.
Heart pounding life, dying to live.

Barabbas, the fall, all with you.
The place null, void filled.
Free from sword, flaming.
At one, mending, remaking, it is through.

EVE

I used to walk these paths alone.
I saw with these eyes all he had done.
I was waiting for something, something so sweet,
and when I first saw you, all was complete.
Walk with me, take me by the hand.
Speak to me; help me understand.
I reach down and cover your eyes.
We hear His footsteps; see His image in the skies.
We spin in circles, dance through the night.
Breathe one breath; one heartbeat, one thought in mind.

Eve
What have you done with my heart, my heart?
Where have you cast my soul tonight?
Eve
How did I stay so blind to it all?
These steps we've taken; one great fall.

How does life go on when
the only way from here is down?
My body buckles when I think of His face.
Things are changing; we're dying in this place.
I reach down, pick you up, wipe a tear from your eye.
We gather pieces of brokenness left scattered by the lie.
The only way, as we make our way now,
is to create our dreams, make it a life somehow.
And Eve, you carry our Hope in your soul.
And for His sake, never let your love turn cold.

Eve
What have I done with your heart, your heart?
Where have I cast your soul tonight?
Eve
How did I stay blind to it all?
We've taken these steps into one great fall.
Eve

KOSOVO

No dreams,
No dreams.
His home is not even there.
How dead can you be,
and still breathe this air?
How many days
can this life pass you by?
Tears cannot measure
how the heart cries.
Success is a word
that just passes by.
Success tonight
is just to survive.

He walks dead;
his spirit taken from him.
His steps carry him southward
to see his children again.
I care for nothing tonight;
no castle fortress on a hill.
But I ask of you,
what no government will.
No dreams,
No dreams.

He runs from the garden,
not staying the watch.
Chains rattle in the darkness,
the wind scatters the flock.
Lightning crashes
over one man's death.
And one man still lives,
having only his breath.
No dreams,
No dreams.
No dreams take away this night.

Daylight rises
with a slow rainfall.
Nothing seems as quiet
as no purpose and no call.
A wild dog howls,
as water drips through this tent.
If we changed places
would it be any different?
For a battle's no battle
unless you must fight.
And the battle that's killing me
is to find your dream tonight.
Let me dream tonight.
Let me dream tonight.

EXIT

Exit

Cold

Conveniently old

Exit

Warm

It's not your time to be born

Exit

War

A political decision

Exit

Peace

Yours is not the right religion

SELF

I was so used to the pull
and the pain it would bring.
So used to the fool
dancing in the rain.
So used to the tug,
a tornado in the drain.
The pull, the fool, the tug of the insane.

What flows as water
once fell as rain.
What opened as a flower,
bent and closed for a hurricane.

What swings the sword
once bore the brace.
And broken noses heal
to lead the face.

The pull, the fool, the tug;
who knows of these in the self?
The side awaits its thorn
as rest is on familiar shelves.

And the foul and the flood
overcome the mornings grace,
and we awake as in birth,
to God's forsaken place.

REVERSE REGRET

Reverse regret,
while possible to eat words, take back time, back-step
       off toes,
salve smooth a soul of a child while mirrors hold you old.
Lines hold the hurts as age with pain softens desserts,
and it all rests in the lap and laughs with the rue of
       hands bent,
and shoulders slumped;
at best maybe that's it.

Reverse regret,
with days being bought, and you being sold, love shunned
       or silent,
and captured in square frames displayed under dust.
Smiles covering all kinds of expression and painting with
       wine those just below the surface in masks, not of
       deception, but in rehearsal
for an unscheduled performance before empty seats
       of audience;
at best maybe that's it.

Reverse regret
while storms lay hold to sand, rocks mocking in the distance,
where weeds choke once vibrant growth and ravens rest,
       bellies full.
Coins stacked, counting alone, their lives interest unknown,
and pleasures expensed, unatoned.
Stillness sits and ponders, not a quiet peace, with voices of
       then and now, reverberating attempts to appease;
at best, maybe that's it.

Reverse regret,
in a place made for falling, a theatre of scarring;
shortcomings the norm, existence, the human form.
Trial and error, the infancy of eternity,
and broken perfection
begs a compass in the cosmos
for a conversation, reflection;
at best, maybe that's it.

Replace regret
What was, has become, through the soil and bloodline,
magnifying the stain placed on life.
No way under or around, there a bridge can be found,
replacing effort and all sorts, examining law and judging
    all courts.
In the place, in the stead, a path erased all steps.
You can't go back, only toward the end: early, mid or post,
    you must begin again;
at best, maybe that's it.

AGE

Age takes me to you my source with a slow vengeance
    of gravity.
Its drag a power not only absorbing muscle and bounce
into a tired stretch and weak hobble;
but also shelving rock and directing tides where to lay,
and pulling desires back into the soul of wistful play.
I lean toward you my little one,
knowing your fresh zest full of fuel for life,
limitless it seems for light.
I am with you in steps taken and medals hung,
with you in your fearless laugh at age,
and such a take at forever young.
The years hold all,
hold tightly the pain of years;
and loosely, all steps and runs and jumps,
though memories, they are here.
So the run then the fall,
the view of you and the champions call.
Then the jolt as sinews meet
the forbidden place where space should be.
Age introduces like a surprise from company.
But I adjust as do we all,
some on couches and some with a fall,
but not to fight for it is ourselves,
though young of mind, our gravity will not rest.
And there you are, ahead of me,
as I try to comprehend the collapse I see.
Smaller hands holding from below,
keeps the days younger for a time.

And then in the aged brow,
there in the wrinkled palm,
in the bent shoulders slumping,
are the child and the mom.
And the two can never separate,
while laughter warms and tears elate,
as innocence aged,
and to the eternal gravitates.

ICE EYES

His eyes ice
His soul
so old
He looked twice
Past the gesture
Past the gift
Of the unknown

What was warmth
Sent the chill
To the spine
And frozen steps
On stone
Stripped pretensions
To the bone

His dark hands
Held relief
But his eyes
A knowing pierce
All of knowing
Not for comfort
But for peace

For unto the least
Is like to you
And the sight
Left an image
Of two needs
Tight-roping
Two extremes

Heat of guilt
Escaping
Through seams
While ice
Through eyes
Saw in me
Frozen veins

FRIEND

Wish u could see what I see
    wrapped in the cradle of a night sky.
A moon as bright as mid-day reflecting off the gulf water
and snow white sand. Stars like diamonds cutting their way
through stone, and Mars red, at least I think it is Mars. Heat
lightning, low in a cloud, fifty miles away and close as skin.
I look down and can see reflection off my fingernails. Man,
it's bright tonight. All my questions, stacked up neatly for
interrogation, melt away at once and I feel no regret.
There are no answers, only realization and its comfort.

A voice soft in the distance; a lite laugh. Life is leaving a
friend, and a friend is there in the gap; a friend of the soul, a
friend for tears, a friend to have. Young hearts weigh heavy in
their youth, seeing the stillness set in. What you're learning
from this trouble, we all will see again. Endless summer
days of sand and salt end in conversations about the days
time takes away, days that cannot be bought. How many
days, and all the shapes a cross can take; each of us having
one, and some carrying one for another; some buried under
the weight, and others portrayed against stormy skies, with
questions hurled as stones that come close, but pass by.

I take your hand and feel the life inside of you shiver, and you
hold strong and close to what is near. It is as if the flowers
that grace and the bouquets that warm, are set in place
and all beauty works to keep you calm. It is as if the moon
is so bright, and Mars so red, and the stars deep mirrors
of diamonds that can cut through the scars of now and
tomorrow. You know the hurt of lightning, ungrounded; you
know it is miles away, and strikes in your soul, grounded.

It is beyond bright.

All your questions stacked up neatly for interrogation, melt
away at once and you feel no anger. There are no answers,
only realization and its comfort.

PRISONER

A prisoner no more,
Freedom is all around me,
No gates, no chains.
A carefree hound
Enjoys his afternoon
Of choices; lay here or lie there,
A carefree freedom.

A cup of coffee
Quakes in my hand,
Unable to rest,
As eyes dart back
And forth, interrupting the peace
Caffeine can bring,
A quaking peace.

Pressed into my brain,
Bar prints that leave
Round molds into folds
Of wave making, affecting
Each twitch and memory
As if it were just happening.
Bar prints as black stripes.

A prisoner always
With freedom all around me.
Seen but not touched,
Not drawn in, not poured
Into a coffee cup.
Once prison has wrapped tight,
To lay here or lie there is enough.

In a Nursery

I say your best will do, then disease ravages like a wolf.
"Floss for the future," then you disappear into the night,
and the world wakes to the fosser's work, but does not notice.
Plan, prepare, pray, then trees fall out of the sky
and replace themselves with you.

Know disorder, know its shape well.
Calamity rests as a neighbor, so love it as thyself.
Lose the fight of nature, its nature is worn hard as hell.
Rock entombed castles, a thousand years may stand,
and one flood, one fire, one movement of land....

You can make no peace with an enemy with no voice,
no hands to bargain, no knowledge of rest.
An antithesis of Theos, wrapped warped into finite,
to undermine the noblest intentions,
and laughter, its plight.

Raven's wolves rest by Odin, cold and longing for the Wild
Hunt across a deadly winter sky.
Who can weather the breath of stars imploding
as if galaxies were lungs;
black holes expiring them to nihilistic ex nihilo?

"Rock-a-bye baby,
in the tree top
When the wind blows,
the cradle will rock
When the bough breaks,
 the cradle will fall
And down will come baby,
cradle and all."
In a nursery,
we were taught it well.

LET THE CHILDREN SPEAK (JUBILEE 2000)

Passing days, wasting away.
A summer breeze, with no relief.
It's not right to be so wrong.
Wanting the fun of a clap,
With no song.
No song to sing.

Let the children speak.
Speak for themselves,
and say the things
no one else dares to think.
Let the children speak.

She doesn't need tomorrow,
just needs to be free.
And today as deposit
on what she can be.

Now princes in castles,
with crumbs on their feet,
Their laughter covering echoes
from the dungeons beneath,
where life, where life has gone to die.

A breadless boy wakes
on a starless night,
to see a red flashing savior
like a penny in the sky.
Take me, take me he cries.

And part of the earth falls,
we think, into space.
But as it spins full circle
as a hand, it slaps our face.
And warnings return, return to the soul.

Let the children speak,
and not with their last breath.
Our fathers passed on,
and our burdens their debt.
And it's growing us old, dying so cold.

A bloody boot,
so neatly has been kept.
And the foot from a neck,
to you, just a step.
And one giant leap it will be.

Now walk down a path
to a cage where you're free,
and ponder the thought,
"what if it were me,
what if it were me?"

Let the children speak,
speak for themselves,
and say the things
no one else,
no one else dares to think.
For one night,
let the children speak.

THE DAY BEFORE

The night before I died
I saw my grandma for the last time.
Ice tea and coconut-cream pie,
it was just the night before I died.

Elementary, long school days
gave way to an existential college haze,
and you drew nearer and as I drew away
and found death wanting the next day.

Wedding bells rang up to the sky.
The songs we sang, there was no time to cry.
And love beckoned to be shown the night,
and was slowly frozen and let me die.

Hands un-held, hearts un-warmed,
days un-lived, gifts un-torn,
truth silent, lies sworn;
conceiving, conception, burying un-born.

Filling the grave with events of the day
and movement retracting life away.
Life on hold, waiting to say,
'I've happened the day you passed away.'

The day before I died,
my parent, brother, sister, cousin, bride,
Pastor, uncle, boss, neighbor, friend of mine;
I was with you the day before I died.

LOVE IS THERE

Love is there,
there alone,
and seldom finds
the warmth of home.
Worlds spin around her
and long for the unknown,
and your dizziness tonight
out of control.

On a starving desert plain
love left, and left remains
Hearts that beat only to measure pain
And hands that grip to stake a claim
Is it love if it's torn away?
Is it love if it's torn away?

The one you look to, hard to find
You search intently with glassy eyes
And one is gone and only the night
Your heart a field, plowed under sky

Explode, and exploded, and explode
And love is there
there alone
And she seldom finds
the warmth of home

THE RAIN

Where is the calm
before the storm?
Where is the eye
of the hurricane?
Can you see what you need
in the depth of the pain?
And you know, you know,
You know the rain.

You've walked these streets
as it's pouring down.
It's life for some,
and for others to drown.
You reach for cover,
some shelter for your soul.
Try to wring out the truth,
that you've lost all control.
And you know, you know,
you know the rain.

Shots in the darkness, shouts in your mind
Nothing waits for you like the passing of time
Hold on to shelter, let go the shame
And let it rain, let it rain,
Let it rain.

No Funeral

We walk these, our streets alone,
past images blurred on dull screens.
You see the movement of death
and strangely, hear no screams.
The unprotected lay still,
held collected in the form of the kill.
Pictures burn in our minds
as evolution breathes its will.

I say where are you my friend?
Too involved to defend?
Too much time to spend
on the traditional myths of old?
The crimson stained soul
of a dream uncontrolled,
floats over open graves
and never looks in.

The lust for your freedom
is ill with illusion;
trusts in your skill
and the art of human intrusion.

HUMANITY

We run beneath stars.
We steer in parked cars.
We survive life's scars.
We dream, can only dream where you are.

A war moved in,
like the righteous in sin.
It drew blood from kin.
We know we may never know you again.

Then a scream,
Like flesh boiling in steam,
Strips away everything.
We try and try to find the Sephardim.

Through a castle door,
down steps to a dungeon floor.
Walls of granite 'round treasures you adore.
Outside, explosions keep you from the core.
Forevermore, forevermore, forevermore.

EFFECTS OF

Vine of life full of blood love;
the kind that screams and dies,
and knows not why.
Tell me why the dizzying spiral.
I'm not alone in this sinking.
There's laughter from the wings
as this tragi-comedy writes itself
at the expense of you and me.
If only forever and not for the moment;
if only the pleasure, but that too poignant.
Created in pleasure and the pleasure, pain.
Dominion over all, and all ends in nothing gained.
So overload the day and rock away the night;
sure that broken laughter fades with the light.
The gaze is for eternity,
the twinkling blink for the sighs,
and the lesson of spring, nothing ever dies.
Just hell for the haughty and summer for the spies.
Where truth is tried, deception sprouts a root
and grows along beside and develops tasty fruit.
So truth with deception, a harvest of all things,
and feasts and winks and screams
inscribe our human names.

FEAR

This is the letter I never opened
And the one I never sent
These are the words never spoken
And the place I never went

The train that was never taken
The guilt that never blamed
The prayer that was not spoken
And the life that never changed

For I have only once to live this moment
Only once to see this day
And the chance that is not taken,
With the sunset, fades away

You're the one I never noticed
Like breath in the cold morning air
You're the walls never crumbling around me
Held by the trappings dangling there

You're the joy I never released
And the friends I never knew
You're the person I've never been
And the things I may never do

I ask that you no longer pass
And I not speak your name
I beg this day not fade with,
'I wish I could live it again'

The clanging of chains around me
The falling of 'ifs', 'could of', and frets
Open a world of possibilities
Where I will live with no regrets

Now the hope that was never spoken
And the dreams that were left unknown
Lay cold, scattered and broken
As blocks to build tomorrow upon

For I have only once to live this moment
Only once to see this day
And the chance that is not taken
With the sunset, fades away

Love is a Door

You are physically and emotionally spent
All that could go, got up and went
Chemically you are ret, mentally inept
The excuses you bet, ran out and yet
Love is a door you are passing through once more

You are hanging up days with the nails of your pain
They hold life tight when you fall again
And you really don't know if you can hang on
Surrender's not a weakness, and your not that strong
Love is a door you are passing through once more

What you've been, you can never be again
What you'll be, you've never yet dreamed
In the blur, you try to focus on the truth
You take what you believe and it's what you always knew
Love is a door you are passing through once more

What drives the wings to soar the heights
Is what shrouds the moon to pale the light
Shoulders so broad, broken before their time
Drinking the juice before it can wine
Love is a door you are passing through once more

Relationally worn
Spiritually torn
The excuses you bet
Ran out and yet
Love is a door you are passing through once more

LEARNING

Not quite strong enough to hold on
Not quite weak enough to let go
The lessons of learning lie in the float
Then the tide rips you again
And the beauty of drowning is learning to swim

SCHOOL COLORS

Cold
Uncomfortable
Imminent comfort
Free
Ease
With less pressure
More noise
I know I shine like a star in the pitch night
I hear low moans
Louder laughs
The dirty water flows down, hazy
Now it's white I see
Tile
Porcelain
I think of the exit
Surrounded by shadow
My face rushing forward
Into the clean white
I leave evidence
Red
Bright
Running down the silver and white
My eyes black
White spots dancing on them
With no rhythm, but constant
The pain suddenly pumps its way
Throbbing
Reminding me to look
And I see the sad dull covered
With gold shining

Mocking a smile
My body breathes
Wreathes in pain
And my movement
Draws out of the gray
An orange flame
Cutting into me
Through pale skin
White
Bone
Freeing me finally
From this carnival of war
I feel sticky hands rummage me
For spoils
And it's green
And it's silver
And I gave it all
Twelve dollars and thirty-eight cents

FALLEN

Looking out from the pain
Looking for the stones to roll my name
I'm hoping that it's you
Hoping this is not all I get to do

And when I am alone
And I'm introduced to myself
Hoping that it's you
Who knows me like no one else

And I've tried and cried and lied
I've hoped and lost and died
Now the last to go is pride, the last to go is pride
And I breath the need, for you by my side

Looking out in the rain
To the cloud pouring down my name
I'm hoping that it's you
Hoping, my God, that it's through

And I've tried and cried and lied
I've hoped and lost and died
Now the last to go is pride, the last to go is pride
And I breath the need, for you by my side

Hold me, hold me in this scene
Hold me, this day in a dream
And it's me and it's you
Elemental in this truth
The loss in this pain, the love in your name

And I've tried and cried and lied
I've hoped and lost and died
Now the last to go is pride, the last to go is pride
And I breath the need, for you by my side

JEREMIAH AND CECIL

There is fire in the bones,
and the bones creak and ache,
the framework of a lifetime.
Their calling fulfilled, yet still,
embers of life and heat,
shared with the shivering,
are white hot and fully effective
to clear forests and level brush,
and crackle through golden fields,
elementally changing whatever they touch.

The fire that has roared is now
in protected environments,
simmering and sheltered;
maybe a bellow for a day,
but not as back in the day.
The fire doesn't explain itself to burning bones,
to sermons silent and quiet microphones.
It doesn't extinguish but burns in the mind,
and the fire that scorched souls
now sits restless and confined.

The work complete, with work to be done,
sees a father pass down, awkwardly,
an uncomfortable transition.
So side-by-side, where one used to carry the other,
the fire wields a bond, as the weight shifts,
one generation to another.
It's a fire that keeps warm the bones,
a fire doesn't leave them cold.
Creaking, aching, burning,
fire in the distance, fire of home.

THOUGHTS

Sometimes my thoughts tiptoe
Because they pass close by you
And you are sleeping and I want
To wake you but the thoughts are not
Quite sure what you would do
Thoughts tiptoe, tiptoe lonely past
Then I see you smile
And thoughts tiptoe back to fields
As they always look in the past

Sometimes my thoughts stomp
Because they pass close by you
And you are deaf and I want
To scream at you but the thoughts are not
Quite sure what you would do
Thoughts stomp, stomp ragingly past
Then I see you confused
And the thoughts stomp with clinched fists
Looking revengefully into the glass

Sometimes my thoughts cry
Because they pass close by you
And you are broken and I want
To help you but the thoughts are not
Quite sure what you would do
Thoughts cry, cry a language of the past
And I see you're listening
And hear the thoughts cry into the dryness
Asking does this pain always last

Sometimes my thoughts soften
Because they pass close by you
And you are forgiven and I want
To tell you but the thoughts are not
Quite sure what you would do
Thoughts soften, soften to pass
And I see you're thinking
And the thoughts soften for a future
Where neither are bound by the casque

CHRISTMAS EVE FIRE

Momma fell into the arms
of her mom wrinkled with love.
Something scorched the future dark,
and nothing remained to burn in her heart.

Though a star was over Bethlehem
and Christmas children were all around,
red flames reached their peak
as black ash settled on a frozen creek.

Days and years crackled,
rising out of sight.
No 'Jingle Bells' to ring this evening,
no 'Joy To The World' to subdue the night.

A split-pine home could not defend
against the fiery decadent;
and the flames would not end
until the horizon flat again.

From a Christmas with no tree,
with a future that was maimed,
a preacher man and his family
can't forget the strength they gained,
when I was only three.

FINALITY

I awoke to the grey, maybe morning
No sun breaking the horizon
No birds of song in the heavy air
No chirps and no smiles
Maybe mourning

The melodies are quiet maybe somber
Resting on this stone day
Not even a dirge to move rested bones
No sound and no dance
Maybe sober

Your song traveled with you, into life
The sun breaking the valley shadow
Imagination moves melody into warm air
A victorious voice resonates as soul
Into light

OF LIFE

He split the rocks in the wilderness and
gave them water as abundant as the seas;
he brought streams out of a rocky crag
and made water flow down like rivers.

PSALM 78:15-16 NIV

"And the ragged rock in the restless waters,
Waves wash over it, fogs conceal it;
On a halcyon day it is merely a monument,
In navigable weather it is always a seamark
To lay a course by: but in the sombre season
Or the sudden fury, is what it always was."

T.S. ELIOT, *THE DRY SALVAGES*

DREAMS

From a distance
Flowers on a hill
Through winds blowing
See them still
And the closer I get
Watch them disappear
No fragrance
Decorating window sill
The rain keeps the colors
Like pain takes a pill
Dreams from a merchant
Buy them if you will
Dreams the color of flowers
Dreams, not real

MOTEK (SWEETHEART)

Smiles and hugs
facades of love
Rose bushes, fresh flowers
cut for the day
While thorns do their part
the fragrance of art
Vases full and faces the fool
and aces the queens do play

Human perception
of loves deception
lies only money deep
I must say
And love is warmer
and stronger and longer
when something else
is at stake

Man the beast
boasts, and the least
lays him to waste
in the lay
And the clock and the turn
the urge and the yearn
the game of the
soft tunnel of play
Release only leads to
a river of needs
that flow with the seeds
of the human traipses

Please, please....

When on a whim
you let me in
the heat of the sin
burns within
It's Him that rescinds
and renovates again
Man's fall not fruit, but pleasure
If not, why the pain
to bring another name
and man's demand to cleave
If not for the urge
and the push and the purge
then nothing's walled the leave

My fall to one
who follows another
is not a portrait of the weak
but the crystal clear pierce
of the alone that is fierce
with desire of creation to fill
And not from the human
but comedy of the rule man
who placed this drama
in the hands of
the out of control
Testing the tested
the jesting of the jested
the mind overlooks or explodes

The thighs only warmer
as the slide in summer
brings this overload to expose
But the battle between sexes
keeps the fool and it vexes
the weakness few overcome

When it's over,
the wise never knew her
The twists and the turns
slow with age and the grey
and the motion of love loses shape
The warmth of the sun
has had its run
and God forbid God behold
the human strength in the faking
It's His drama, the element of karma
he so patiently covered with grace
What a theatre to behold
all he has allowed us to mold
and to shape into this confusion
We are pawns with a promise
with the power of limitation
that constantly cries to fly
We are placed in this experiment
where love can be spent
as redemption for sins
that the weak just might

I'll take your love
and help from above
for all the things not right
Things I didn't create
the apple and the mate
and the desires of the human plight
It is my shame and you take the blame
as I fall into humanity again tonight

STEP INTO DAD'S SHOES

I step into my dad's shoes slowly,
one year at a time.
He certainly has not outgrown them,
but the bends and curves and scrapes in them
seem even more familiar than those in mine.
The prints they've left in years,
not so distant from today,
and they were new in a different world,
with less thought of comfort, more of work than play.
Is it to fill them, in this changing of the guard,
these ones whose steps have been firm,
whose paths have been hard?
With steps taken to carry, and strides toward celeste,
laces now tethered more closely home,
and loosed with more intention of rest.
No, never to fill them,
but to know what moved them with motivation for the door,
what they protected in all elements,
what news they moved forward for.
It is in the preservation of these worn soles,
their gift still giving to the ends of the world,
that souls are known in songs of ascent
on paths that angels tread.
I step into my dad's shoes slowly,
one year at a time,
and know they are renowned for landscapes covered,
and wonder how they ever became mine.

THE THOMAS IN US ALL

I think what matters is the smile on your face.
I think what counts is the time you didn't waste.
I know what hurts is what can't be replaced.
Love shines, its shadow, a countenance warm in Grace

When the questions swim larger than the answers we know,
move the real to the middle against the flow.
When signs and times and leaders turn cold,
the leather bound grounds heavier than gold.

Those that can't be answered weigh heavy on the mind,
while the air in our lungs never crosses our minds.
The miracle of ru'ach, a humbling sublime,
as skin stretches to dirt under parting ticks of time.

To know in part, and to fully understand,
that part is what we've got, a partitioned land.
The smile of obedience in the innocence of the lamb,
is to hold on to what's not yet, to be unfolded into the plan.

I think what matters is the smile on your face.
I think what counts is the time you didn't waste.
I know what hurts is what can't be replaced.
Love shines, its shadow, a countenance warm in Grace.

PLAYGROUND

Ah, landscape, the only difference
as swings and sun and shadows
act as a mirror of memory,
yet right before me.

The soundtrack of laughter broken
by small streams of mixed joy;
but laughter wins the day.
Knowing the days are endless,
until you're nearer the end.

And there I am, forty days or years ago,
only, maybe better, and curious
with love I never knew existed.

All of heaven in innocence;
the eternal laughter of heart.
The joy of not knowing
that wounded and broken branch,
its fruit tainted, its taste stench.

Never hunger for the fall;
never cross over the bridge.
Your eyes, still of creation,
your breath, still of the evening walk
Your purity in play, still knowing a Father,
still in the coolness of the day,
still hearing your name.

Have all swings, sun and shadows.
Have all laughter, curious with dance.
In the wind, your heart to Him,
and joy be all your chance.

Ah, landscape, the only difference;
a mirror of memory right before me.
With a stream of mixed joy,
there a father and there a boy.

Vaux's Swift

The Vaux's Swift in mid-flight
glimpses treetops like daffodils
as they break the light.
The summer wheat, a golden treat
to the Vaux's Swift in mid-flight.

Summer's liquid mirrors
reflect the arrow's movement
of life passing in clearer sky.
Lakes then hills, lingering by thrills,
then valleys to echo the cry.

Soaring or'e lanes,
connecting the paths
that lend stories to fleeting lives.
Where men chatter, children yell 'batter'
then listen to tales of wives.

A partial viewing
of fractured memories
laying on stone as offerings.
Broken by cloud, like a friend allowed,
in small towns on quiet mornings

The winged missile sings
tires, and yet remains
and knows its journey will end.
So much that's free, and still to see
even as the flight descends.

VOLCANO

All and everything,
there pushing down, down and in;
inside pushing in, pushing till smoke.
Jostling from the outside, the weight and wait.
There, mixing the foreign fires,
assimilating with the unconquerable,
now inseparable, the compound and swirl;
the elemental nausea of spin and tilt.
Heat flees for the hell too hot,
and the pushing, mixing, spinning seethes.
There's no return of lines no longer crossed,
but melded from soul into soul expired.
The heart of the earth troubled,
knowing that crashes explode into crashes
of light and power and expanse,
giving way through brute brawn the mother life;
to son and sun, eliminating the impure
and refining to liquid platinum
at the expense of all that's not;
all that burns, fades, withers, dries, dust.
At a point of tipping from the bottom up;
beyond boiling as the rumbling growls.
Knowing that the coalescing, the igniting
lasts into nights, weeks of nights, then years.
Then years and a lifetime of heat, seeing red,
losing with time the layers of life real, but peeled to the core,
and it, liquid emotion as lava plays its creative role so well
as destroyer and paver of new roads, empty.
The roaring dragon draws from the belly its fire of Vulcan,
and its life a spewing furnace entering

the parting and surrendering atmosphere of blue and breath.
The pushing pressure reversed upward into a war
    of landscape,
carving the earth's detente,
drums ceasing under the wind's flute with a dirge and dance.
In them lay the quenching, as the Lucifer turns to black soot
in the cooling, and either victor, scarred or vanquished.
And with the morning's sun,
a light on the scars that are carried eternal.

REQUIRED

Tonight it's required. It's required of you tonight.
The world, the callouses,
the stained refined chemical element of
atomic number seventy-nine.
"Arrange them in two stacks, six in each stack, on the table..."
What burns away in the heat of the fire,
it's there as requirement.
Bring in the broken, the pool is stirring.
Drown the paralysis in the flow of creative fluid,
and feel it float like stone, like the substance of the heart.
The temerarious trait human in nature bubbles forth,
speaks from the inner chambers and is pulled to judgment
as blood to oxygen, its creative source.
Tonight, the wellspring requires the return of its flow.
Water forms walls, water from rock,
and water a path for faith to have stepped out on.
Tonight it's congratulatory.
It emanates from actions recorded and steps ordered.
Tonight, it's all that is gained that is required.
Arrange them on the table, all that is gained in one stack, six
as its number, and in the wind breath, the essence of spirit,
weighing the twain to see what was gained and what was lost.
Tonight, that is required of you.

Leviticus 24:6 NIV

WINE AND PSALMS

A bottle of wine and a book of Psalms
lay by dusty feet and in calloused palms.
I make a toast like I'm giving alms,
raising the wine, praising in the Psalms.

And like he danced, the heart fully exposed.
In all this chance, the mind fully knows
that a book of Psalms and a bottle of wine
is the path of success to the heart of the Divine.

RU'ACH

The air, still as a frozen memory,
locked in squares on dusty shelves.
Bouncing in minds, remembering,
or confused with time.
It is air that brings life to the scene.
Breath, wind, spirit.
All decay starts when it leaves the room.
He has left the building,
like a mighty rushing wind.
We are somewhere in between.

PERSPECTIVE ON BEDTIME

She replaced my brother.
He used to lie next to me at night;
his cold feet grazing the backs of my legs.
Her warm back now exciting the sleepiest of nights.

I would jump and holler,
"fish feet, get your fish feet off me"
"fish feet," I would call them.

We now talk late hours of childhood pranks
and joke and laugh and drunkenly slumber.

He would laugh and haw and plan his next attack.
She clings and cries and rejoices with peaceful sleep.

Different lives it seems to me,
the companion and the need, both indeed.
And I wouldn't trade this moment for another,
a childhood with a brother,
and a lifetime with my lover.

WEIGHTS ON A BALLOON

Like weights on a balloon,
these days to my life.
The winds right for flying,
the wings silent in the night;
the bells chime of duty,
and ring 'responsibility';
trapping the body to the ground,
while the mind soars the seas.

The clamoring, the hammering,
the ringing and the roar,
deafening, but not as severely
as when loneliness encroaches the door.
And the wait is in silence,
and the weight is in gold;
the dreams less dangerous in youth,
than when cast to the old.

When losing the way, the day,
the fight and the score,
you may count it as victory,
if it's Truth you're fighting for.
The ascension to mourning
from pushing through pain,
into the brightness of morning,
having lost all for the gain.

Like weights on a balloon,
these days to my life;
to anchor the floating
and focus my mind.

WINDS OF CHANGE

The winds of change
not always in a storm,
but in the soft breeze,
constant against the moor.
Silver linings
grey into dull;
a ship's spirit pirated,
its treasure sunken, its remains, a hull.

In the setting of the sail,
lay the counting of the cost.
The direction of the pull
leaves other lanes lost.
The depths no longer matter
when the sail is over many leagues.
The safety of obedience obsolete,
with no captain and no king.

The salt, a savory savior,
burning as it heals.
The wound of a ripped voyage,
quenching a thirst as it kills.
The wound, the blood, the scars;
the fade of innocence into reality.
The joy in abandoning destruction,
bubbles with the seafarer's gurgle,
"I am free."

HENRY

In a coal mine mind
he raised his eyes above
He smiled goodbye to a world
that showed him no love
The mountains lost another soul
as the rain fell on stripped land
Black roads lead to a white bed
where chunks of life, like coal,
fall from a mountain man

Sing his song tonight
Tell a tale that won't be told
Sing a line from a life
that's growing old

Too many people
in too high places
demand too much
from cold black faces

Trying to hold on
He just held out like the coal
Till a winter storm blew
and he learned to live in time to go

Sing a song tonight
Tell the tale that won't be told
Thank you for my father
From your life that's grown old

HONEST EDGES

How honest can I be
and not lose a friend?
What if I died for you
and couldn't rise from the dead?
Job was the hero,
but not the goal of this life.
Deserts where we banquet
and African, the skies.

No one good, no one honest,
no one crawling from the sea.
Hands holding hope broken,
not reaching you to me.
Torn the picture
of a picture perfect scene
Blood in the pitcher,
poured in disbelief.

The tale of old told
while ears ring with sleep.
The other side of love shallow,
the other side of numb deep.
Can emptiness save the day,
asks an empty-suited soul.
And reasons fly like bats
into a narrow hole.

Love crawls, falls, and tumbles down;
scratches to the surface to try again.
Its blood-curling, righteously selfish scream,
pulls the eyes and at the heart of selfish men.
Enough of enough,
slim the mirror, foggy the view.
And too much of not enough,
off the wall, off the cuff, edges of you.

Maybe a friends dying,
the death of a deal.
Spokes turning in a circle,
seeking a path, searching a wheel.
Hands held like breath,
turning blue in their grip,
as a wave in its depth
pulls a current to a knot that doesn't slip.

CROSSING THAT LINE

Age acts out its play right before our eyes,
has taken a thousand days, wrung them tight, their dripping,
    moments of melted life.
Age, the warrior, and such loses no fight.
Youth like guests slowly, unnoticeably leaving
    in the steamy night.
Each day goes, but goes into the next,
where memory confuses adolescent fire
    with embers still in the mix.

What it takes leaves a crease to hold
some stories written down, some laughs linger uncontrolled.
It's victory as a grandparent in peaceful panic through a
    cracked megaphone blaring relic,
While the coming of age drowns the wind in the sails of
    a mighty ship adorned, all the day surrenders to its
    crossing of that invisible line which is only realized when
    it's already behind you.

MOTHER

You wake with a morning smile
feeling the world is going to change.
The planets spinning, lining up
but the universe, not the same.
A flutter, like a butterfly,
the light wind of a breeze.
A tickle, on the inside,
a little dizzy, then to your knees.
Your heart pounding, your mind wondering,
My Lord, is it to be?
That the soul of a new child
has traveled here from eternity?

And the awe of it all
in a moment, coming to be.
The gift that is this life,
desire into reality.
You might be the mother,
the warm life to the son;
you might be once barren
but now you are the one.
There's crying in the morning
then laughter in the night,
as the stars twinkle majestically
over the birth of new life.

CHILDREN

Your hands small and soft.
Your heart strong and sweet.
Your mind, as the morning sky,
curiosities colors painting deep.

The lines in my hands
may be a path for you to know.
These hands that hold and shape you
and prepare to let you go.

Love walks between the steps
of a father and his child.
Late nights, laughter and dancing,
the years, only a little while.

In all these efforts to grow you
I still fail to be fair;
knowing I can't always hold you,
I can always hold you in prayer.

Our days aren't the same,
but I live some through you.
Your innocence before our father
a valley snow, a mountain view.

Flesh of flesh, my blood,
the closest, next of kin;
knitted together, though separate,
in the Son, we begin again.

And my life is not my own,
I lay it down one day at a time,
for a Father who gave His child,
and for this sweet child of mine.

In Between

A child's dream
while lying in a field,
becomes a man's canyon
and the dream still real,
just falling,
rocky
and broken.
And someone's trying to do something
with plans that open to nothing.

A man hammers
down his own home.
He worked so hard
to be so alone.
A child
crying,
wanting to know.
And someone's singing his own tune,
not quite sure of the right cue.
Just asking,
have you
stood at the door?

Love doesn't come
for cheap or for free.
It reaches in deep
and pulls the air from me.
It is the hardest,
and easiest
choice.
And everyone sits in silence.
In the silence, does anyone hear a voice?
Whispering,
in between
your lives?

THE ART OF GOING ON

I balance this silver spoon
and the malice comes with truth.
You look through a man's eyes
to see into his soul.
It is an art,
the one of going on.

While you balance your life
between two ways to die;
born on the wrong side
of the earth's spin one night.
It is an art,
the one of going on.

Can I not meet you
somewhere in the middle,
to relieve my conscience
and your hunger a little?
Have we not met
in the reflection of his eyes,
and of all our differences,
one realized?
Art is in leisure,
and an art to survive.

HIWASSEE

Some sweet night
you'll dream you are a child again.
Needing no sunlight,
not wondering where you've been.
You've watched innocence
lost with no cause,
and no love
can bring you round again.
Some sweet night
we'll dance; we'll dance as friends.

Tell me what got you through,
sometimes loves not easy to bear.
No one would call your name
or reveal they were there.
Silent enemies entrenched,
plans made with no thought in mind.
Peace comes with a price,
and for love, maybe a lifetime.

Some sweet night
we'll dance at the river's edge.
Some sun so bright,
we don't see the ledge.
A mountain train carries your dreams again.
Some sweet night
we'll dance, we'll dance as friends.

COLORS COVER BLACK

Colors cover black
in a room
where two worlds attack,
with dreams
carried on the other's back.

Manicured existence,
while smiles
hem in the resistance,
with life
protected by the assistance.

Cover up a wound
till it's
covered up with a tomb,
and memories
passed around a room.

Made for a mission
in a cave
where votes secure religion
with razor ladders
for the jump into division.

And we swing
from side to side.
We lean
from innocence to pride.
And we hide
in the details of this life,
and lose
no sleep tonight.

Colors cover black
in a room
where two worlds attack,
with dreams
carried on the other's back.

EXTREMES

Do you ever hear the silence of
what remains from a broken love?
What is passed from father to son,
and knights April the cruelest month?

Try to listen to what's not said.
See how the heart turns the head.
Sweat like blood, drops from the dead.
In silence, to the slaughter led.

One extreme of the sun is silver,
one extreme is gold.
One extreme of life is murder,
and the other is growing old.

I have stumbled, tripped while alone,
fallen beside, truth as a stone.
I have spoken to one who's not there,
in curses of anger, with tears of care.

What's not, becomes real
when thought becomes word.
When the mind is not spoken,
there heart can still be heard.

And one extreme of the sun is silver,
one extreme is gold.
One extreme of death is life,
the other is to not know.

LAILA

Middle school songs to sing along,
Her spirit singing in the wind.
Her eyes searching the crowd,
And smiling to take it all in.

Her cheeks like laughter,
Her laughter like grace,
Her life like love,
Forever on her face.

Skating the ice like wings take flight.
Her years full of sacred dance.
The stage holds her hand, spins her again,
A stage to live out all her plans.

She glistens on ocean waves
To reach and paint our sunset.
She sees all of her days complete,
And not one will she ever forget.

What was so near was the eternal,
The song and the laugh and the dance.
What she knew was to love, and now
She and God give us that chance.

St. George

Life,
it just seems to pass you by.
Old friends
seem to disappear in the night.
I have stood
on this shore before,
twilight
and all the things I adore.
Warm breeze
blowing against my skin.
Calm sea
calls me home again.
If I could
slow it all down one day,
this would be
the way I would want it to stay.
You,
walking in the sand.
A little girl
reaching out for my hand.
Tall ships
passing by in the distance.
Daydreams
coming true in an instant.
I believe
If God were looking for a place
to open up
and show his face;
if water
were to be his voice,

this island
would be his choice.
And dreams pass through a man
like water
moves through sand.
And hope
is a dream that's real,
and teaches
the heart to feel.
I say
"Let me dream tonight."
He says
"Let your dreams be your life."

SUNRISE

Sunrise,
sunrise over the sea.
Twilight,
twilight, there's a memory.
I've been on the water,
I've lived my days as a boy.
I worked the shorelines,
the high tides
and the dry times.
I've been rich,
I am poor.
In the twilight,
it's just a twilight memory.

There's a new moon
setting in the east;
a warm breeze
moving through the trees.
I've worked with my hands,
not wanting it for free.
Knowing God gives
the life I've gleaned;
a bounty.
I was rich,
I am poor.
In my twilight,
it's just a twilight memory.

WE STAYED

A breeze blows
the sea breaks.
I ponder what it takes,
to save love
with mistakes made.
A vow to keep
and never break.

The sea and sky
meld into one,
and sand washes
warm in the sun.
Two lovers move
in an embrace.
Weather worn,
not torn,
face to face.

We stayed, we gave,
pushed thru the waves.
We tried, we cried,
and it never died.
Nothing's been harder,
sweeter or stronger.
And I'm glad to say,
we stayed.

A babies cry
and sleepless nights,
turn to little leagues
and pony rides.
School plays
and parent nights,
prom dresses in sunlight.

There was love from mom
and fairy tales.
Advice from dad
and wishing wells.
Both were there
with time to pray.
What to do and what to say,
in the struggles of the day.

We stayed, we gave,
pushed thru the waves.
We tried, we cried,
and it never died.
Nothing's been harder,
sweeter or stronger.
And I'm glad to say,
we stayed.

FLUIDUS,
THE FIRST THING I REMEMBER

The first thing I remember
when I was only three,
was standing by the old barn
in a field with my puppy.
Then flashes of childhood
run like rushing water,
starting slowly,
then a turn, twisting,
rolling over death so near.
Boulders waiting only inches
below the surface.
The wind and water
push me somehow
for a short time
safely over what
I see not and fear not.
There's somewhat of a calm…
Endless, endless afternoons.
Warm, warm sunsets
casting long, playful shadows,
flowing into silhouettes
moving in the low light of the moon.
Hours of laughter echo,
sometimes with tears,
into the next game.
The stream becomes a river
before I can tell it's changing;
deeper water and more danger,

less innocence but protected
somehow, with more knowledge
there seems to be more fear
and less known
about what to do about it.
Life smells the breath
of death and dances
a dirge.
So little is assimilated.
It is profoundly experienced
and at the same time,
for experience's sake.
I turn, turn away, turn to;
take the hand of tomorrow
and try to hammer the happiness
out of a new attempt at life.
Somewhat, yes, more aware,
but ignorant of the abilities within
to reach goals that are yet
to be set.

The river widens
and takes on new character.
The scenery, much different.
So much must have passed
while I was not looking.
I float through images
that are only familiar

to me through the
lives of others.
Those who made it this far
are strong, must be strong
or mad;
maybe too weak to end it.
I see above my presence
and I envision the river
ceasing to exist
of its own definition,
disappearing into
the great depths of
the raging body
which swallows all waters,
and slows the rushing
into a to and fro rocking
as if to lull a child to sleep.
And it takes the slow flowing
mighty and it thrashes it
into the air and
bashes it into the rocks
bringing torrent and confusion,
calming and destroying.
I lower my head and swallow.
The water burns my lungs.
I see many familiar faces.
I see weary bodies
and creased faces,
cracked hands
and bent backs.
I spit it out,
as much as I can,
but the salt taste lingers,
creating thirst

in the middle of flood.
I reach and reach and reach.
What for, what to?
Something crosses my hand,
breaks the skin.
It feels so close
I try to cling to this rock
that I know survives the deep.
I sense the hope,
remember food for a hungry man,
a prayer for a crying man,
his family tragically taken.
A smile crosses a widow's face.
Carols are sung,
a child is protected and loved.
Water crashes against the rock.
I lose my grip.
My lungs burn;
the unexpected pain,
I swallow again,
hoping for air.
I go down twisting, turning,
trying to find my way up.
I am thrown into a rock
below the water,
a last hope, last chance.
I swallow, choking,
clinging to the rugged
but solid surface.
My hands are torn,
Eyes can't function,
but burn intensely.
Holding on is the hardest thing
I've ever tried to do.

To let go would end it all.
And holding on...
And holding on will...
And holding ...
I swallow
And pull up.
I can sense the horizon
beginning to lighten.
I hold on
and swallow.
Laying on the side of the rock,
asleep,
dreaming a small puppy
is licking my face.

BIG WORLD

It's a big world that we live in
But a small room where we sleep
I can spin around the world in a day
And never leave my seat

> There are bright lights
> big places
> sweet dreams
> fast paces
> But it's a small place
> where I lay to sleep

I can see the past from where I lay
The big events that have led to this day
All of them much bigger than me
And it's a small place where I lay to sleep

> They are creation
> the fallen man
> salvation and
> the coming again
> But it's a small place
> where I lay to sleep

Voices calling from this world, wide open
So many diamonds in the coal of the night
Castles on land bought with other men's dreams
But it's a small place where the prince lays to sleep

He's out there in any given place
In the picture of famine I chose not to taste
In the dying desert or in the house of greed
It's a small place where the rich and poor sleep
Into the worlds of men let me go
Let me be taught so that others will know
Know that soon we will all reap
And that it's a small plot where we will all sleep

There are big dreams
old age and youth
life and death
and the hard truth
But it's a small place
Where we lay to sleep

STILL

There is a confusion that comes from knowing
and a hunger from being full.
A conflict within your peace
and a wellness that leaves you sick.

A man curls up beside the child inside him
and they look at the world through one set of eyes.
The trees around them see so much smaller
than when he could see years into the skies.

And life carries with it a need to die,
like shears pruning away the thorn.
And death carries with it a place to lie,
Leaving layers that can't keep you warm.

What I knew I have forgotten.
What I had has floated away.
What I dreamt, I saw in the day.
And in the silence, I heard him say,

It's a journey, don't be in a hurry;
fulfillment cannot be complete.
In this turning still a yearning,
still bitter in the sweet.

Now climbing around these stairs,
a curious circle to the stars.
And skeptics sit at different levels,
and proudly boast, 'we've come this far.'

Sad ones falling to the left and right.
A taste of glory, a turning away.
In this turning, still a yearning,
still darkness in the day.

AUGUST EVENING

August evening,
summers leaving
and life feels like a breath.
Could be any year,
could have happened anywhere.
The circle has never changed.
A friend called
just to say
a friend is here to stay.
Through thick and thin
Count 'em in
when so many have walked away.
And here we are
again tonight,
blindly setting our sights.
And near the desert
children cry,
cry themselves to sleep tonight.

Warm
Warm blood through our veins
Walk
Walk slowly by the remains
See
See the faces with no names
Know
Know in his eyes we're all the same

Tried to stay,
love of yesterday
before an old man walks through a door.
And then again
I scratch the skin
of tomorrow to see how it bleeds.
While strangers call
from under their wall,
one, with a lifetime, they can't scale.
And we as strangers
to another who lingers,
and hear faint cries in the night.
Remember now,
realize somehow
that now is what we've got.
Summers leaving
on an August evening,
your lifetime, your one shot.

SUNSET SKETCHES

Sunset sketches
Days like witches
Flying past.
Out there, somewhere
Sweeping it all away.
Dreams like water
Move you a little farther
Home is a place
We try to be.
Moon disappears
Like childhood fears
We move from behind trees.
Sun rises with hope
That faith will cope
With what
Destruction has created.
Building a world
That spins, but it twirls
Headlong to the future
Of all that's hated.
And sleep needs rest tonight.
Cloud covering clears
Revealing all the years
As a lone hand reaching wanders,
'In absence, have they grown fonder?'

1978

I met my brother
In 1978
We were on our way to school
We were running kind of late
He said I'll be leaving soon
But I won't be gone long
He left later in the fall
And I'm still waiting for him to come home

I thought I saw my brother
While riding on the train
The doors slowly opened
He was slumped over, shivering in the rain
My stare increased intently
I saw a memory etched into his pain
I stood slowly to walk to him
Only to have the doors between us
Cruelly close again
A childhood for a brother
A lifetime that's not the same
I saw him in '78
And he'll be home one day

Family Farm

A little farmhouse
A little girl standing in the field
Wide-open dreams and wonders
With all the love a little heart can feel
She remembers the words of grandpa
And the times he used to say
'There'll come a time when you'll be leaving,
I just didn't know it would be today'
These fields have moved under my feet
These trees have blown through me
The waters of this rippling brook
Have moved my spirit to be free
A movement in the moonlight
An auctioneer puts labels on our soul
How will there be a new beginning
When all that's worked for has grown old
Life is nothing to hold on to
Falls like a snake from your hand
Passes like clouds in the night
Moves like water over sand
The future is for dreamers
Do you see it now or not at all?
A little girl thinks she'll make it
She's not sure about grandpa

TODAY

All the movements of a
Soft poetic dance
All the debris of a
Gone bad romance
Closets made larger
For skeletons to dance
Fear made smaller
Truth into a trance
What can be, is what is
If you choose to make it so
Your chances scream 'take me'
Your dreams from melting snow
Too much of the future
Seems too close today
Too much of the past
Has moved too far away
Too much tomorrow
Too little today

OVER LOVE

Over love
Clear glasses ring
Clouded with deep color
Nature's blood
Deep with life
Over love

Hands reach
And pull away

Slowly,
Rising
A small circle
Becoming less fixed
In the blue-white
Whiter,
Then sky
Spiraling upward
Always a fog
With shadows of it within
Disappearing, and followed
Leaving itself
Left like cold wax
That seeped into cracks
Filling a void

Lips part
Words somehow escape
There's the cool
With lips left

To be seen
In the air
When glasses ring

Words somehow escape
As part of my hand
Is part of my face
And life is in the breath
Which is over love
Mixed with death

Through a small window pane
Feeling a comfort
From the autumn rain
Clouds slowly moving
Leaving a shining cover
In the pre-dusk
Surrounded by conversation
With subtle laughs
A small disturbance
Overlooked and past

The cling is right
The mood is in nature
Creativity is formed
Carving a path
Between the words

Leaning,
Reaching,

Almost awkward at first
The goal in the haze
Seems attainable
By the drug
In the stench
The desire
To hear stained glasses ring
Over love

Jesus, Do You Know Me?

Jesus, do you know me?
I think about you frequently.
What then do l owe you?
Nothing down here comes free.
I used to try to see you
almost every day.
Now I catch a glimpse on Sunday
in a different kind of way.
I've moved across town,
changed jobs and settled down.
I have a wife and small family,
I don't know if you would recognize me.
I'd like to have you over
to remember the good ole times,
to talk about the future
and a few things I have in mind.

      Oh, you say you've seen me.
      I didn't know you were there.
      You were waiting in the distance,
      trying to catch words of my prayer?

Oh, I'm sorry, I didn't even notice you,
I must have walked right by.
You should have called my name
or spoke a casual "Hi."
Oh, I'm sorry about the noise,
it does get loud at times,
but will you sit down now
and let me look into your eyes.

Oh no, don't go yet,
we've just begun to speak.
And I've been thinking
I'd like to see you more than once a week.

> You say I can do that,
> but wait, why must you go
> Oh, you say that you will lead
> And that I need to follow

But what about my family, my job,
this place and my chores?

> You say they're really not mine,
> but all this is really yours?

But how can I let it go?
How can I give it all away?

> You say I must trust and believe you
> each moment of each day.

Whew, that's amazing!
I just asked if you knew me.
I don't know how this happened
but you have seen right through me.
What do I do now?
I've made my life such a fuss.
I can't keep living alone,
Hey, wait up, Jesus!

ABANDONED

Is there love for you tonight?
There's none left here for me now.
Twenty-two years of my life given
is not enough to keep you somehow?
"For twenty-seven years," says mama,
"he kissed my cheek each day,
and now that my children are grown,
through a door he has walked away."
Why have I given you my life?
To watch thirty-two years go by?
We should be laughing together,
We sit in different worlds and cry.
Twenty years is like a lifetime
and for twenty years I gave my best,
trying to build my life around you,
now its crumbled into hopelessness.
For four thousand years I spoke strongly,
and for two thousand now, I've shown my love.
You're not the only one to feel abandoned.
Without you, it gets lonely above.
Understand unity is a God-thing
if you are going to make any union succeed.
Love was made in My image
and was broken on a broken tree.
And when you walk away
from all that He is trying to do,
you break into pieces,
not knowing, only He has life's glue.

THE UN-LIFE

What was free, you did not take
What cost the world, you ate and drank
When you saw, you closed your eyes
What you knew, you didn't realize
All you have is now broken
All you love is now cold
All that's aged, longing for youth
All that's young, growing old

THE DEATH OF A SEA SHIP

Struck by a force that had once carried
      me around the word.
Cool water once cleansed my appearance
      Now it rips my skin
      My insides bursting out
Such a friend, but only for a trip
      The trip is now through
      I creak and reach for you
      My sails see no shore
You are only water, choking, letting in my death
      I try to buoy once more,
      But you're so cold and deep

Bury the sea ship with no stone
      And no story
Only a memory of a Gulf Coast morning
      Where men are happy and free
      On the same peaceful, deadly
      Waves of your sea

SOME THINGS

Some things do not mix
Oil and water
Man and Divine
Thoughts and reality
Memory and time

Some things do not separate
Blood and water
Man and sin
Dreams and disappointment
Never and again

POP AND THE PINE (FT. DESOTO)

Green with life, gray with age
Giving mercy from the sun
Arms stretching out
Balanced between
Home and the sea
Echoes of laughter
Under your shade
Resounding a child's innocence

The sea paints itself forward
Your branches swaying,
Circulating the salty air
White salt chalk remains
As signs of the tide disappear
Gone is the sunset, and you with it
Lunar images become clear
Stirring memories within our hearts

The story remains
And in your breeze
We still hear the tales
Days of outlaws
The sea and its bounty
Comedy of mistaken identity
Early days and rough times
That calloused hands
And of laughter that
Kept hearts soft
Family, honor and honesty

Tales were fabricated
And some stretched
All to tell a truth
That finds in all of us
Resemblance of life's
Gradience and grace

And in your rustling
We hear his laugh
In your swaying
His theatrics displayed
His stage once portrayed life
Upon your ground

I cannot look to you
And not see him
I look to you often
His spirit in your wind

DESTINY

After the whistle blows
the head pounds with papers, missed appointments.
Voices echoing shallow sentiment,
and growl, not for losses
but for earlier roars
and ones to come.

Don't shoot!!
Don't shoot!!
Is it possible that if you do not care
you can live longer?
What is it if you keep yourself
and strive late nights with words
and not with laughter
so that achievements are made,
and completion occurs?
Storage is brought from nothing
to be filled with all the things you need
but can never find.
And do you give it all
hour after hour,
day on top of day,
year by year,
till your pockets are full and fat,
so that in a second
as you hold your breath,
one greasy soul-less form
that lives a bastard life
raises his pride to your head
and laughs at the years of your toil;

makes mockery of your early rising
and spits on tomorrow,
staining the wool and stretching the fibers
until they snap, each, one by one,
taking in an instant
what has been nurtured for a lifetime?
Are you to break out of the cycle into life
and have the cycle break into that
and take you back by force,
screaming and crying, kicking, aching
bleeding and dying?
Taken back home, stretched out
with holes in your body,
open and unprotected by your Rembrandt
hanging slightly crooked
by the opening of a door.
A faceless, organic portal is seen by all during dinner,
strolling into his concrete cave,
cringing not at all the echoes
of doors and bars and lifetimes closing.
He goes in to hibernate,
to await another spring
when the hunting will be good.
His presupposition concerning
the lack of his life
keeps him from fearing losing it,
and he winces not
at the thought of leaving the dead-end
and trying something new.

You are this striving soul
that is wounded and dying and dead.
And you are this detached piece of hate
floating in society, waiting to attach
to the more fortunate in any sense.
The decision lies before you each day,
and it is a difficult one,
the decision of destiny.

Fighting a Lie

There's nothing harder to fight than a lie

                                    It can change shape at anytime

It can surprise you or knock you blind

                              Nothing is harder to fight than a lie

That's why you don't fight it

                                    You watch it from the side
See it change shape, wither and cry

                              Surprised by its loneliness,
It is bald-faced and blind

                   And if you don't fight it, it will subside.

CHURCH

'Kids, get ready for church'
I heard every week growing up
A clean shirt, don't be late
Sit down and straighten up.

Mama sang, Daddy preached
And we all sat in a row
Heaven and hell, right and wrong
Learned most everything I know

And now I know
And now I know

Up at six to go to work
In the fields that were my home
Summer break on grandpa's farm
The hardest work I've ever known

Help a neighbor and a stranger
Never give up, never give in
Was a right way, made you stronger
And salvation for your sin

And now I know
And now I know

There's no price for what they taught me
On mountain roads, by rivers banks
They say nothings owed them for this love
But through my life I give them thanks
Through my life I give them thanks

Well these times have passed it seems
And children keep growing up
But don't forget the love they need
The kind that's kind of tough

And what they might not know
As they wonder this world and search
Is the truth their hearts long for
Might be found in a little church

So Let them know
Let them know
The truth their hearts long for
Let them know.

WASTE A DAY

Don't waste a day he used to say
As we scattered off, bikes rolling and laughing
With time ticking as straws in the spokes.

We were too young to know or notice
The years dropping off, hearts beating and racing
And youth to old as age to our folks

The wasted day always there for play
As unworn fetters rested in corners dusty,
Unnoticed purpose ignored as pinkies hooked for promises

Only experience could teach, so a prayer for each
As words from a pulpit fell,
of science and faith resting chalky on green behind roses

What did we learn, something to earn
As we brushed the side of knowledge
Getting to the other side, not knowing the passing of destiny

The day and the wasted day,
The future not the same in deserts to protect you
Children play as God would have, and the rest age to gray
     in antiquity.

DISTRESSED LIVES

Distressed lives
Stretched over wire barbed
With purpose of hanging days
pulled and pierced
Sinful to the end
The end of repetition

Joy moves quickly, surprising the day
And long afternoon sunsets, seconds
Pain struggles to outlast light
Taking black cloudless pitch,
pronating the breaking dawn
The dawn of deliberation

The thorn deeply successful
Twisting and turning, the side carries its weight
Fights until sleep conquers the day
The evolution of rest, calm in its wind
The stillness, mysterious movement
The movement of all to the sea

Conversation with Self

If you think being yourself is hard,
Try being someone else, it's impossible.
If you're ever lonely, think of God;
He thinks of you even when you're not lonely.
I think people get mad at themselves
for lying to themselves
just like when someone else lies to them,
it just takes a little longer, and the blame is spread around.
I don't believe a coffee bean can save the world,
but it can save the morning,
which most people care more about.
When I watched my grandparents grow old,
it was really different than watching my mom and
    dad grow old,
which for the life of me, can't be what I'm going through.
Would you please stop giving me opportunities to
    forgive you.
And always remember, a human body
has a human being living inside of it.

3 AM

The loneliness of 3 am is so loud I can't sleep.
Words chase thoughts around my head trying to trap them
Under the fog that keeps my eyeballs afloat.
The man-made air brushes over my skin like a razor blade on
glass, just uncomfortable enough to accentuate the gifts that
keep me awake.
I am reminded of half a world with no moon
And half a world that is always awake.
I think of children who play until sleep overtakes them
And 3 am is a mysterious place they can never find,
And I chuckle to think that 3 am overtakes me
And my mind is 3 hours early for its appointment with
daybreak.
Those who sleep evades and horizontal thinking entertains,
Join the stars in twinkling or tinkling,
Wondering where the last cookie or astronaut went.
3 am and space, related, distant cousins,
The one that was never quite right.
I'm happy that he visits
And that I awake just in time before he goes away.
He never speaks but brings thoughts to a groggy sleep,
Just enough, like he is saying, "I'm here, look up, it's 3 am."
The cold reality is I have to sleep to be awakened,
Have to wear out to miss half the earth's spin,
To be unconscious to dream, and struggle to see at 3
By the luminary that reflects thoughts,
And warms them back to sleep before the breaking dawn.

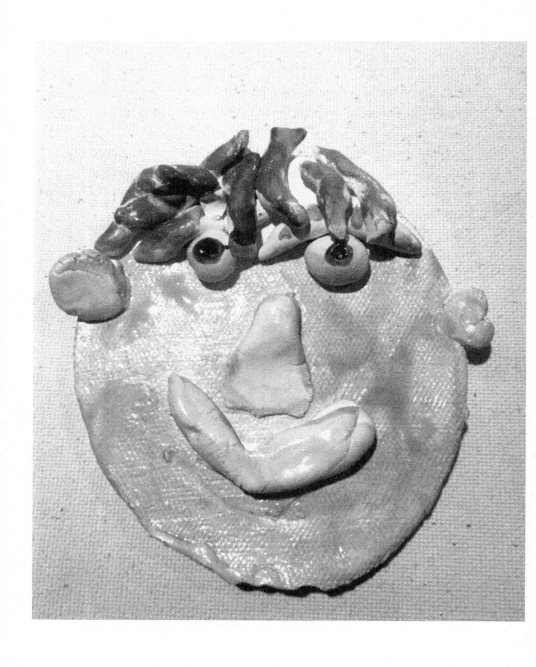

OF LAUGHTER

"There was one thing that was too great for God
to show us when He walked upon our earth;
and I have sometimes fancied that it was His mirth."

G.K. CHESTERTON, *ORTHODOXY*

"If you want to tell people the truth,
make them laugh, otherwise they'll kill you."

OSCAR WILDE, *THE NIGHTINGALE AND THE ROSE*

THE BEANING OF LIFE

It's early in the morning,
the alarm goes off.
My head hurts,
I'm walking around the room like a lost dog.
What went wrong in my life?
I got to face a day,
hadn't even finished the night.
What can I do,
my eyes like zebra stripes in a zoo.
You looking at me, I'm looking at you,
you're feeling it to.
And we say well, well well...
And then there's a smell.
And it's percolating,
and my whole body says it's been waiting,
aching for what's making.
Get the sugar get the cream before I scream,
awake from a dream.
Everything's changing and it's not just me,
the whole world's waking up, waking up,
waking up to a cup of coffee.

Maybe it's heaven in a pot,
maybe it takes you a double shot.
Maybe a mocha, a frappe, a latte,
I can't say, but I do pray
for coffee cake, can't be late.
Maybe it's venti, or a soy chi grande,
maybe it's black and hot at midday.
But when the caffeine hits my veins,

I feel it ease my pains,
and I'm ready to take the reins
thru the air, on water, in trains
And stevia, sugar or splenda
is better than a smoothie in a blenda.
You can take my coke, my water, my tea
but you better not, and you don't,
and you won't, and you better not,
you better not take my coffee.

Now it's afternoon,
I'm running behind,
trying to get to the carpool line,
get the kids to practice on time.
But my energy's in decline,
feel like too much wine,
my lids close like I'm going blind,
so I can't wait.
Need something to help me see straight,
to get home before too late,
get dinner on the plates,
lift some weights and find what motivates.
So it's straight to the drive thru
for a fresh hot cup of brew,
and I wave cause I see you're human too
and I think what can we do and be,
it's all cheap but it's not free.
And we raise our cups for all to see
that we run, we work, we thrive
on a bigger, better, fresher bean

for a bolder cup of caffeine
And it helps once again,
helps all it can. It's coffee.

Whew, I made it thru another day
and I feel great, going to stay up late.
Watch some HGTV or the Office on my HD,
running on energy that I can't see
but it's inside me and it's time to be,
so it's just you and me.
You looking at me, I'm looking at you,
you're feeling it too.
And we say well, well well...
And then there's a smell.
And it's percolating,
and my whole body says
it's been waiting, aching for what's making.
Get the sugar get the cream before I scream,
awake from a dream.
Everything's changing and it's not just me.
As the whole world goes to sleep
we're having an after dinner,
after dinner, midnight coffee

BREAKING EVEN

I have fallen behind
and there's only forty years to catch up.
Sounds like a lot of time,
but I'm forty years behind.
The first forty,
a wild rushing wind.
Found salvation
and learned to sin again.
If I get there in time,
it will be the finish line,
and the forty years of meaning
will have me just breaking even.

ALWAYS

Always went looking for something
that if you think about it, probably didn't exist.
But always was persistent
and would never relent.
As he went along he met sometimes,
with eyes glistening in the sunset,
which changed his whole point of view,
having now been introduced to regret.
He held on tight to never
like he had never before.
He was pondering his dilemma
when he heard almost knocking at the door.
With fear and doubt, he wondered about
what may be waiting outside.
Then continued, with maybe later,
a conversation that seemed to never die.
With half a mind he decided
that always is who he is,
and nothing could stop always,
except never, his next of kin.
Now always and never
struggled for years it seemed,
while sometimes and almost
worked their way in between.
Then maybe later and regret
lost interest in the fight,
and took up with two losers,
maybe not and might.
Always is now tougher,
much more the worldly wise.

He knows he's seen nothing,
unless he has seen both sides.

Now always sits alone
having been that way for a while,
weary from the resistance
in going the extra mile.
But somewhere, somehow,
something's gotta give.
While the grave's gravity pulls,
Always always strives to live.

Plan B

They say time is money
I say that's a joke
I've got all the time in the world
But I'm always broke
I'm looking at plan B

They say there are some things
You can never know
Well if that's the case
How do you know?
Looking at plan B

They say time will tell
But what can it say
As I stood here listening
I lost another day
I'm counting on plan B

We stood out in the rain
Waiting for fairer weather
But no one hears 'for worse'
They only hear 'for better'
Now there's always plan B

They say time will heal
There's truth in that ring
And since you left me
I can't feel a thing
It's time for plan B

So I dropped my thesis
In the kitchen sink
Halted my career
Just to have a drink
Got so low
I had to get high
Now it feels so good
Just to get by
I'm living on plan B

You say you want to spend time
But it's money that's spent
My times too expensive
So I had to quit
Now it's on to plan B

They say take your time
I say take it where?
So I went to find time
But it was just not there
So I'm counting on plan B

They say there's lost time
But where did it hide?
Time waits for no one
Right when I needed a ride
Gotta have a plan B

They say time flies
I say, 'I'll go along'
But I couldn't find time
So I'm flying alone
It's part of plan B

They say we waste time
Like your love on a shelf
But we don't waste time
We just waste ourselves
And move on to plan B

        Well, I dropped my thesis
        In the kitchen sink
        Halted my career
        Just to have a drink
        Got so low
        I had to get high
        Now it feels so good
        Just to get by
        I'm living on plan B

Now, someone said you can kill time
And I said what would you do that for
Of all things to kill,
That's the one thing I want more
Even on plan B

SPIRITUAL BREWERY

I think Jesus would have a enjoyed an ice-cold beer
He liked boats, nets and fishing gear
Spent some of his time chasing hogs,
Knew the crumbs from his table fell to the dogs

He chose to serve fish at his big picnic
And kept his boys close, real tight knit
He hung out with a rowdy crew
And I think he would have enjoyed an ice-cold brew

Now some may think his taste too fine
After all that water turned to wine
But it was his mother who egged that on
And people talked it up long after he was gone

He said "if any man thirsts, come unto me"
I am your spiritual brewery
If any man drinks, he'll thirst no more
So fish from the other side, move the oars

Boats and men, battered and tried,
Sails worn and knots tied,
Judas cussed and Peter lied
Beer iced and fish fried

Now know a new day will come
When sin's no more but there's still fun
In a place improved but much like here
We'll sit with Jesus and have an ice-cold beer

MARGARITA

Here we are again,
Margarita
Just you and I my friend,
Margarita

I once said this must end
But that must have been to your twin
Now it's rendezvous again
Margarita

My hope was to move on
From the coolness of your song
Now I've been with you all night long
Margarita

Oh, Margarita
We've been together so long
You keep me hanging on
Our frozen love is so strong
Now it won't be long till
Margarita

You've always been there for me
Even when I couldn't see
Keeping my hour happy
Margarita

Now, can you hold me anymore?
Can you show me to the door?
Is there time for just one more?
Margarita

Maybe now is the time for 'I do'
All my friends, they do approve
I think they're in love too
Margarita

Farmer's Daughter

From Florida she came
and from Virginia he went,
in Tennessee they met
at a college where they were sent.
Now their backgrounds were ideal,
the intention here is not pun,
for she was a farmer's daughter
and he, a preacher's son.

He went there to study the word
while only a teenager.
But when he saw her lovely fruit
he had to change his major.
She showed him around the garden
and of its beauty, he remained impressed.
But she said, "Wait, love is patient,
It's not yet time for harvest."
So they buckled down and dreamed about
the future they could share together.
The fiery sword of the word of the Lord
and bumper crops in fair weather.

The first time he met her dad
he told him to have her home by eight,
and since it would be after dark
he shouldn't plan to stay.
So he figured out a way
to make dad think things were fine;
he brought her home at seven
and stayed till half past nine.
Now he is truly thankful
the farmer's daughter became his wife,
for she is always in season
and her love is always ripe.

Daily they're spreading the Gospel
as they raise Cain each night.
She is his farmer's daughter,
she is his lovely wife.
And the missionary goal
is not the only one,
when you're playing in the garden
with the preacher's son.

FOR YOUR COOKING

Autumn air without a care
Saw your face and had to stare
There was a connection to your complexion
And it caused an immediate reaction
The way you moved had a groove
Had to get to know you real soon
It was then and there I stopped lookin'
And told our friends a wedding was bookin'
And before too long we were hookin'
But baby, I didn't marry you for your cookin'

It was for your eyes, not your homemade pies
For your touch, and not your soup n such
It was for your shake and not the way you bake
It was for some fun, not your hot-cross buns
And what keeps my attention, and to you lookin'
Guess what baby; it's not for your cookin'

We settled in right and fine
Days were a feast and nights were wine
Love lasts even when the belly growls
And on peanut butter and jelly we survived somehow
Late night snacks kept us alive
Sweet like honey and bees to the hive

The kitchen remained quiet and clean
We knew dinner was ready when the doorbell would ring
But with time, the way some things do
The love stayed strong, and the cooking talent grew
Now kitchen life is awesome, though funny, it's true
She makes great aphrodisiacs and we rendezvous

But baby, I didn't marry you for your cookin'
It was for your eyes, not your homemade pies
For your touch, and not your soup n such
It was for your shake and not the way you bake
It was for some fun, not your hot-cross buns
And what keeps my attention, and to you lookin'
Guess what baby; it's not for your cookin'

THE BOTTOM OF A BOTTLE

Where do I find
A friend so fine
One that's all mine
Not at the bottom of a bottle

Where can I go
To seek and know
Something to show
Not to the bottom of a bottle

What can I hold
To love and mold
A warmth from cold
Not the bottom of a bottle

Where to be free
And not worry
Were eyes aren't blurry
Not at the bottom of a bottle

What about a mumble
To fall down and stumble
Have my thoughts crumble
There, in the bottom of a bottle

How about to invest
In the future of a mess
And when, is a guess
There, at the bottom of a bottle

Three sheets to the wind
The quench of a blend
The overachievement of sin
There, on the bottom of a bottle

To sit and ponder
This fruit and wonder
The proper behavior
Staring at the bottom of a bottle

So, the time I'll pass
And sip from a glass
That taught me at last
To stop before the bottom of a bottle

Pentecostal

God gave us chicken for fryin'
God gave us breaded pork chops
God gave us bananas for puddin'
But He didn't give us hops

He gave us California raisins
From sweet grapes of the vine
The delicacy of grape jelly
But He didn't give us wine

He caused us to shake, quake
And fall into a trance
To run the pews, roll and shout
But didn't allow us to dance

He called us to rock a thons
And lock-in, sleep-overs groovy
Spun us round skating rinks
But never could we watch a movie

He guided our paths to summer camps
And Camp Meetings in the heat of July
With goulocks, gauchos and stiff blue jeans
We were allowed to fry

No beach, no shorts
No rock-n-roll and no beer
No long hair, except in a bun
And no shiny things in your ear

But there was one sin that was allowed
As we gathered around the table
Of chicken, chops and nana puddin',
saints could eat as much as they were able

Now most of the norms have faded
And the memories not that awful,
Of the bellies and chins of members and friends
Who I grew up with as Pentecostal

OF AMERICA

"We shall be as a city upon a hill,
the eyes of all people are upon us."

JOHN WINTHROP,
FUTURE MASSACHUSETTS GOVERNOR, 1630

"We laugh at honor and are shocked to
find traitors in our midst."

C. S. LEWIS

CRACKER

Rockin' chair
Black boy
Swayin'
Old door
Creakin'
As it swings
Some fat lady
Singin'
Old man suit black
Preachin'
With a bent old woman "Amen"
Sayin'
Rusty 'Coca Cola' sign
Hangin'
A clickity old truck
Missin'
Wine-lipped street bum
Stutterin'
Tie chokin' shoes shined
Spittin'
Skinny mixed mutt
Howlin'
Some domestic love life
Shoutin'
Distant gunfire
Ringin'
Toothless wind blowin'
Whistlin'
Bloody fight loser
Leanin'

Over chairs
Fallin'
Low cut calico
Teasin'
Words in the haze with forgotten
Meanin'
Ripped into the wind rain
Freezin'
Fought them damn Yankees for no
Reason
But this is our town sleepy
Dreamin'
Ole Reb still hangs high breeze
Wavin'
But over two races equal
Mixin'
Our change gilding
Changin'
Ropes lay dry still stretched from
Hangin'
All shadowy mysteries keep you
Guessin'
Cream of the crop from bottom
Risin'
Waitin'
Hopin'
Tryin'
Till White House and black man
Combinin'

A Place We've Never Been (9-11)

Freedom found
by the shore,
a small town
being born
by the sea.

And without freedom
in the beginning,
this life
would not be;
but now found on the wings
of one and a million dreams.

Now in a city
that never sleeps,
Lady Liberty bows to weep,
into the sea, her tears falling.

And the city lights
by night, illuminate again,
the strength of the nation
she lies within.
Brother, sister, God and man,
hero and victim, hand in hand, tonight.

And faith
will rise above.
Our spirit, like a dove,

reaching a place we've never been.
Love growing strong,
children hanging on
to a strength, making us strong again.
We are free,
we are free;
and it doesn't,
no, it never comes cheap.

In an Eastern
sunrise sky,
we see the devil
behind hollow eyes.
We smell the stench
of his breath,
his faced scared
with lines of death;
and he slithers out of control.
But his hate
is suicide
imploding his own mind,
and he wreathes to know
freedom won't die.

And survivals not
what we're for,
nor the glory
of necessary war;

but the revival
of the spirit of man,
to defend truth
and believe it again.

Now, though we feel
a nation mourn,
we will not die
but be reborn.
And now the city
that doesn't sleep,
mirrors a courage
our nation keeps,
to boldly let
freedom ring
as devils bow
to Sons and Kings.

And faith
will rise above.
Our spirit, like a dove,
reaching a place we've never been.
Love growing strong,
children hanging on
to a strength, making us strong again.
We are free,
we are free;
and it doesn't,
no, it never comes cheap.

BUFFET ON DECEPTION

Now that sin is legal
we move on to grander schemes,
Above the truth that binds us
to the death our pleasure brings.

We make conscience an outcast
and wait for echoes from fallen walls.
We sleep outside cathedrals
and worship in government halls.

If we haven't found it,
we say it isn't there to mention;
and the questions become the answers,
and each his own redemption.

Lies are for sale
and they're not very cheap.
Costs you more than the truth,
and when you've paid, still can't keep.

A man on trial for murder
begs his accuser for the call,
"Am I tried for a crime
no longer gracing the court's wall?"

We buffet on deception
and diet on the truth.
Fools lead like kings
and make mockery of sooth.

BLIND FREEDOM

Freedom brings with it
The right to lose it.
Freedom is tough enough
To handle your daily dose
But it doesn't hold up
Under your irresponsibility.
Unlike a mentally drained spouse
Ignored beyond uncomfortable,
It will not lay before you
A pork chop and baked beans.
It will not hold your bottle
Of belittlement
As you starve your faithful hound
Lying in the corner
Who has guarded you in your
Forgetfulness for years,
Kept your doors locked and
Watched as wolves walked by,
Their breath fogging the frame
Of your very existence.
This dying friend sees how your
Hands can't hold all that you carry
And yet no crumbs fall from
Your table, a vacuum.
No, freedom leaves that scene slowly,
Like a lost love at celebration feast
Knowing that the room is fragranced
By your behavior and no account
Taken to see what it shows to the door
And out windows and up chimneys.

Laws and love lean to other rooms
Of courteous kindness,
And you do not notice any change
Until your laughter swoons,
And you are hollow with the knowledge
That you were the only one laughing.
The hall now abandoned by objectivity,
And reasons for forgotten friends to dance
Have all been reasoned away.
Yes, you have your freedom now,
It's all yours and no one else's.
But you have purchased it below face value
And it is yours only, no other knows your freedom.
It will not leave you but clings to your sole soul.
It knows only you and
Can never show you anything outside yourself.
Your freedom is trapped within your desire
And your cause, and it encircles your mind,
Coloring every thought till tainted
Is the only color you know.
You may never know your freedom
Has taken your life, fenced out your friend,
Fed your ego pseudo fruit,
And found you wanting you know not what,
Knowing only that freedom is not what you've got.
Now, freedom brings with it
The right to lose it.
Freedom is tough enough
To handle your daily dose
But it doesn't hold up

Under your irresponsibility.
It looks outward, it reaches to edges,
It dips oars and not anchors.
It searches for that invitation of individuals
For it to be and be taken seriously.
But be careful around it
For it brings down walls and fills trenches,
And buries hatchets and any hands still clinging to them.
It opens doors and halls of courteous kindness
And celebrates its character
With the laughter of friends
Around a banquet table of pork chops and baked beans,
A hound chewing the fat in a corner.
It is he who uses freedom to fight freedom,
That loses all his rights to freedom
And makes a prisoner of himself.
Let freedom ring.

THE ANSWER

It's not the answer
we are looking for.
We are looking for a way
to be the answer.
It's not salvation
we are looking for.
We are looking for a way
that does not need salvation.
It's not a creator
we are deeply searching for.
We are searching deeper
into creation for that to adore.
We are not looking
into our hearts for the pure.
We are looking into mirrors
to make sure it's how we look.
It's not a surrender
of the spirit that enraptures our days.
We surrender our bodies
to angry thorns of the flesh.
It's not tomorrow
that frames our minds.
We eat, drink and are merry
one day at a time.
It's not that we are eternal,
and bought at an infinite price.
It's that we're human,
fallen,
half way home,
with atonement as our voice.

SOLDIER

I was only eight years old,
a flag waving in Momma's hand.
A parade of soldiers marching out
to a God forsaken land.
There was my friend's daddy,
he winked as he passed by.
Always longed to see him again
but that was the last time.

For freedom, for country,
for the love of this life,
he was willing to go and pay
no matter the price.
And his days and nights turned weeks to years,
his burden, the weight, of fighting these fears.

Now I'm standing here
in dress blues, smiling at my son.
Knowing it's for his freedom
that I pick up this gun.

I salute the flag
and its glory,
protect these people
and their story,
and know these colors don't run.

For freedom, for country,
for the love of this life,
I am willing to go and pay

no matter the price.
And my days and nights turn weeks to years,
my burden, the weight, of fighting these fears.

We think of Chief Petty Officer Mason,
and of a Corporal named Lutz,
Lieutenant Schwab from Nebraska,
their sacrifice for us.
We stood against the enemy
as brothers and friends,
and now we'll stay strong
to face this enemy within.

For we know it's not freedom
if it's not worth the fight,
and this soldier's hearts for freedom
to make things right.
In the sands of a desert,
to the ends of the sea,
we were born for this time
to keep men free.

For freedom, for country,
for the love of this life,
we are willing to go and pay
no matter the price.
And our days and nights turn weeks to years,
our burden, the weight, of fighting these fears.
Our burden is great, our reward is near.

RED SILVER

Days decay
and the rubble blows in the wind.
Every season
reaches closer to the sleep.
The classes grow apart,
both death to the other.
Two lives,
two lives within the borders.
Liberty is proclaimed
while truth has lost its name.
Mud is all around; thrown mud.
Speak of justice,
throw the facts in his two-hundred-year-old face;
freedom has broken his back
and paper is the law, justice.
Peace cries, peace cries a war cry.
Reality screams out from the blue-scarred
love chasing death as an escape.
Old men cry and wish for death
more than to have their youth.
Mysterious days shape the future.
A dark cloud hangs
over this desert mirage,
and the minds of men
break by the weight of fear.
Evolution cannot save our children,
a ripped generation;
an obese, drunk generation,
walking to the slaughter.
The land dies butchered and stripped.

Men perish
refusing to show the face of honesty,
and Sodom held more glory.
A glass nation must scream
its own shattering destruction,
its face ripped off
in its own destruction.

THE HISTORY OF MY COUNTRY

green grass

gray skies

sand

washed down

sunburn

open wound

blue

worn down

wooden door

train ride

rust

frontier

small town

open plain

gold

sewage

waterfall

desert life

metallic

ammunition

seasons

gray streaks

bloodshot

assault

costly freedom

tough choices

acceptance

suicide

withered

hollow

dry tears

eulogy

Pseudo Pious

Hope comes to America
In aims to retrieve the prodigal
Kissing a disease in San Francisco
Forgiven by the inadequate forgiver
Justified by the adjuster interpreter
Without justification
Upon a rock, a rock of sand
The rock is a ring
But there is no scar on the bearer

Breath and feeling and fight
Are a Christmas morning subject
Given, it is always giving
And why does the screamer
Or in silence, the wise
Forever wait another spring?
From the Fingertip; from the creation of seed,
It becomes the center before there was a barrier
Leb; Owr; Vehement; Eschatos

Lightning flashes as quick as death
Rocks are split, sap is boiled, busting out
"Did God say?" and "Where are you?"
Between these there is no pad for a heel
Weak is the seven a week
Brought home to a smile in plastic cheeks
Decisive the gleam of the straight-forward look
A hero lives death over a plug pulled
Oozing, flowing, expiring as an escape is run

Water on our forehead cannot then
Be expected to bring a blessing
Outside the heart
Water cannot be as a tree
Bearing predictable, obvious fruit
But it flows deep
Piercing, blessing the hearts of men
Deeper than any extension that climbers minds can think
Sawed off, shot down, rung in shin; self questions self

Boots or bear feet
The youth make their choice
Only ten short suns for warmth
A heartless eye and Beelzebub's voice
Like pulling a year from yesterday
The wave of hands cannot be loosed
Seven, holy seven; the eagle flies low
A generation is come with nowhere to go
Walk alone little boy
As the other half must unfold

ALMOST IMAGINATION

One day
this tree will be gone,
grandpa won't be home,
twilight will dim the dawn;
it will be better or worse
than you thought it would be.
It will be,
one day.

Too much
of all this is ever known;
assists us all in being alone,
focuses and rejects the unknown.
Maybe he will not believe
your existence in His imagination
in fact is,
too much.

Freedom
is actually a place,
inside, and difficult to trace,
without evidence, body or face.
The chains that hang, pull and dangle
hold the captive to his choice captain,
believes hope is
freedom.

Sitting near
where we all want to be,
only an image of what we want to see.
We stumble o'er clues around the missing key.
Skeletons shiver by a small ember.
A single flame nearby thaws and melts
life into dreams,
sitting near.

2000

It's the turn of the century
There's no turn of the heart
The spinning arrow falling
As it misses the mark
The death of a country
The dying of its soul
A replacement of the heart
Tickers its weight in gold
Just another day turning
Running away from home
Lincolns at the theatre
Will he ban the gun
Stars hung for worship
Stripes to kill all you can
The spirit storms horse-like
Over faces carved in land
Heroes can't help you
If you bury them too deep
Like dreams that are only worth
The time you are asleep
Paths like words
Written on the land
Civilization like scars

On the countenance of man
We die looking back
On all that has been
We see forever's mistakes
Just to make them again
He's not a joker
But he's on his last round
And when you see his back turn
Breath, like ashes, falls to the ground

We've Come this Far

Global warming scheme
Hurricane warning ring
We pour our garbage into the sea
Diluted atmosphere
Pollution everywhere
The ocean turns castles to shanties
Acid rain
Flooded plains
We've made controlled burning a crime
No herbicides
No pesticides
But human waste on foreign soil is fine

The things that don't quite make sense
Leave the two sides at arms intense
I don't believe we can destroy or save this earth
It is dying and begs for new birth

El Nino
Sub zero
Where California used to be
Plane crash
Blown cash
We crawl to the altar on Wall Street
Injustice
Among us
The earth's lean always favors the east
WW
JD
Is your truth setting you free?

We've come this far and now this
Two sides at arms intense
And progression regression
With no safety in numbers
Unless you're government
Desperate nation
Drowning Haitian
History is the future,
Just stolen
Boring thrills
Warmed over chills
And we offer a lapel ribbon as a token

Truths around
Lost and found
And being wrong's okay
if you're sincere
Stolen chair
And silverware
And our leaders blindly bring up the rear
We look confused into a mirror
Today's choices made fifty years ago
Our reflection blurs a little clearer
That the rehearsal
Is daunted as the show

YOUR HEART MATTERS

I fight the future, like I swing at butterflies, batting my eyes,
and there they are, the years right beside the fears crossing
        the line, and I laugh to know we're this far behind.
Born here, under attack, born there and taken back,
and Moses in the palace didn't dream of dancing in
        the desert;
took lashes to compassion to get retaliation
and reaction and lay evil on its back, broken.
Then forty quiet years till a gnarly bush burst to flames
and the Word was spoken.
'Go back, go back, the closed floodgates to open.'
You fight the future like biting the stones you walked over on
walking over here, and there it is, the hate right beside
        the fears crossing the lines of compromise, but the
        compromise of lies
leads to Devil's eyes, where truth is exclusive
but you wouldn't know because you won't use it.
Base your base on your face,
not the masquerade of human charades;
but you base your hate on race
when your own parents have two different faces.
What color is your heart? The color of hate?
Have some grace and stop trying to take this place
to where there is no hope in the days.
Your selfish greed and thankless heart
trace the outline in chalk on a concrete city maze.
Nothing frees a man like the discipline of his heart and hand
to commit to the working of a plan that fools do not
        understand. Instead you say 'I am, I am,' and your soul
        splits in this blitzkrieg

of the image you were made in,
and you break all mirrors reflecting your sin,
deaf to the earth's cry to begin again.
I AM says "I AM " and you refuse to bow,
but you stand defiant because you are the man,
told so by your serpent with a plan,
and with knowledge you can, you can, until you can't,
which is where we are my friend; you can't.
Can't you understand you can't.
It takes a deathbed heart transplant,
it takes your surrender and your recant,
not your aim at shaming another man.
Don't continue this pathetic attempt
that should insult your intelligence.
It's a self imposed form of bondage
that free men know doesn't cause freedom to grow.
Don't let the liar lead you back through
to lose what you've conquered and know to be true.
You are not a man based on the color of your skin,
what more can give in this country where we live?
Everything is now legally correct,
but it's not legal to demand and require respect.
Keep fighting your way through the paper maches
of stuff that's free and give it to me.
Keep stealing your TVs while your government blames
        the police
and the shortage of trees and big SUVs.
While they fly over seas to pay the enemy
instead of praying for peace.
The enemy is now within, the hatred of truth has let him in

to fundamentally transform what has been.
Only you can be the one you were created to be.
Don't fall into the trap of this deceiver we see,
who has prayed down the division he now seethes.
Use your freedom to love others and respect yourself,
and humbly bow before God and no one else.
You are his image, would He act in the way you are
    now going?
Follow His ways of knowledge,
stop fighting what you can never win;
turn your heart home again,
and start knowing you're a man based on your heart,
not the color of your skin.

No Vision

Change is permanent in a cold needle prick
In a bullet's path from politic
From a missile in a nuclear sky
To a breadless boy who watches it fly

From an alley disease we protect our kids
And destroy a baby before it lives
We teach survivors to find their own way
Then make it crime if they choose to pray

As human bone, stench, and misery
Cross our satellite screens
Send a dollar for conscience sake
And dream sweet satin dreams

GOD REST YOUR SOUL

Thoughts of you lay deep in the souls
of dreamers, thinkers and believers,
who risked so many things, their lives not sparred,
to walk toward you, though you were not even there.
Just the thought of your Life, Liberty, and Pursuit of
Happiness brought estranged souls, prayer-bearers,
freed prisoners, and Lords and Dukes
sailing salty seas to see what chance looked like with a
blessing.
What an imperfect crew that came looking for you,
wanting your gold and treasure
needing your freedom and heaven.
Not all steps taken here were of a righteous man,
but righteousness was written in the hearts of heroes
willing to die for thoughts that declared freedom
dripping from the quill held in brilliant hands.
You are an idea that challenges man's fall,
asking humanity to stand as free men
not bound to selfish law, but selfless sacrifice
for a better place for all.
Not all started free, but a cruel process
started a flow of consciousness
and won the day for your freedom to grow
beyond all homelands that were left behind,
and now you offer those most persecuted
the most opportunity for redemption and reward.
Though many scoff at your unprecedented favor,
their vision skewed by selfish ambition and false premise,
they can't find you anywhere else in the world.
This scoffing brings a pseudo guilt for sins committed

by races fueled by greed 200 years ago.
These cannot even pay for their current guilt
but want others to pay for ancient guilt,
even as they try by giving up more and more
of what was possible on your land.
Your freedom is not dying.
It is being denied and denigrated.
It is being choked by laws and held ransom by traitors.
And now you are being attacked from within,
the enemy hardest to defend.
A progressive plot to undermine what brought
you into existence is underway.
A fundamental change per say,
a changing of the guard with no guard, no hope and no way.
Blood is on a march to your soil
and this time it is to annihilate what is your core.
For freedom no longer rings freely.
Wise and brave men call it an evening
as your enemy comes in to meet
the welcoming arms of those who want your defeat.
The sad day reveals
that your freedom
was used
to kill
your freedom.
America, may God rest your soul.

New Freedom

Of men and their actions
Words bleed out
Syllables not retracting
With the flow of wounded conscience
And with starch white walls of cardboard
While pressing sophistication
Degrees hung
Barns enlarged
Foundations for expression are poured, spilt
Clean and close
Arrogance comes even as sweat from pores
Pouring out promotion, elevation, escalation,
Disillusionment

"And why should not I
contend that the means justified by the end
are not but directions in my hand
to be revealed, detailed by the enchantress
of my own wisdom?
Why should not I
a decision make
when such questions lie in a place so great?
For in me have been stuffed
theories, conflicting philosophies,
knowledge of the enemy
and great elements of these.
So I, correct in politic,
cast my vote unattached,
unaware of my attachment."

From day to night
From a talk show
From sources with power
Or it seems so
The land breathes heavy
Wanting to stop the smoke
Newness is a desire
Change is the goal
So shockingly cold is the lack of goal in the change
Paper foundations result from ignoring,
Denying, falsifying, lying
The script is complete
The players in suit
The setting conditioned
Life is ready to be presented
Ready to move on
The action now taken
Characters are separated
Once loved, now hated
Here come the pieces
Of what once whole
Now severed
Fire fills the eyes
Screams try in vain of wine
To cover lies
Like floating
Feeling of wreckage
All ports of harbor
Have been turned away from
And now in deeper water and less hope

Blood drips down the school's lone steps
Follows a trail home to the projects
To parking lots of fancy and fair
And with all else taken out
Bullets fill the air
Time, thoughts and actions will be filled
On one hand or with the other
And now without peace
Open to whatever
A barren womb
Once carried home
Without a tomb
One of her own
A million more, one by one, choked out
My hands too tired and I, too sick to count
For freedom was cried
As the slave in conscience knew
And all were dying
In the holocaust of the Jew
All being ripped, arrested in progression
Nonviable blood flow
Thick in a downward direction
A staining of sanctity
Has brought actions permissible
In the code of non-ethics
In the lack of commandments
Before the board where all is seared
Where the sacred breath of life
                    Is held
By the choice of new freedom

"He went and lived . . . by the lake . . . the Way of the Sea,
beyond the Jordan, Galilee of the Gentiles . . . From that time
[he] began to preach . . . As [he] was walking beside the
Sea of Galilee . . . [he] said, "Come, follow me, and I will send
you out to fish for people" . . . They were in a boat . . . and
immediately left the boat . . . and followed him."

MATTHEW 4:13-22 NIV

CPSIA information can be obtained
at www.ICGtesting.com
Printed in the USA
BVOW03*1951101116

467522BV00003B/4/P